"NO DEPOSIT, NO RETURN"

Enriching Literacy Teaching and Learning Through Critical Inquiry Pedagogy

Jennifer Aaron ■ Eurydice Bouchereau Bauer ■ Michelle Commeyras ■ Sharon Dowling Cox ■ Bren Daniell ■ Ellen Elrick ■ Bob Fecho ■ Jill Hermann-Wilmarth ■ Andrea Pintaone-Hernandez ■ Elizabeth Hogan ■ Hope Vaughn ■ Amanda Siegel ■ Kathy Roulston ■ Hernandez

INTERNATIONAL
Reading Association
800 BARKSDALE ROAD, PO BOX 8139
NEWARK, DE 19714-8139, USA
www.reading.org

The International Reading Association attempts, through its publications, to provide a forum for a wide spectrum of opinions on reading. This policy permits divergent viewpoints without implying the endorsement of the Association.

Director of Publications   Dan Mangan
Editorial Director, Books and Special Projects   Teresa Curto
Managing Editor, Books   Shannon T. Fortner
Acquisitions and Developmental Editor   Corinne M. Mooney
Associate Editor   Charlene M. Nichols
Associate Editor   Elizabeth C. Hunt
Production Editor   Amy Messick
Books and Inventory Assistant   Rebecca A. Zell
Permissions Editor   Janet S. Parrack
Assistant Permissions Editor   Tyanna L. Collins
Production Department Manager   Iona Muscella
Supervisor, Electronic Publishing   Anette Schütz
Senior Electronic Publishing Specialist   R. Lynn Harrison
Electronic Publishing Specialist   Lisa M. Kochel
Proofreader   Stacey Lynn Sharp

Project Editor   Amy Messick

Cover   Design, Linda Steere; Illustration, Photodisc Photography Collection/ Getty Images/Veer.com

Web addresses in this book were correct as of the publication date but may have become inactive or otherwise modified since that time. If you notice a deactivated or changed Web address, please e-mail books@reading.org with the words "Website Update" in the subject line. In your message, specify the Web link, the book title, and the page number on which the link appears.

Library of Congress Cataloging-in-Publication Data

"No deposit, no return" : enriching literacy teaching and learning through critical inquiry pedagogy / Jennifer Aaron ... [et al.].
      p. cm.
   Includes bibliographical references and index.
   ISBN 0-87207-583-4
   1. Literacy--Social aspects. 2. Critical pedagogy. 3. Action research in education. I. Aaron, Jennifer, 1972-
   LC149.N6 2006
   370.11'5--dc22
Second Printing, July 2006   2005030599

We dedicate this book to our past, present, and future students for whom we hope these investigations through critical inquiry are and will be a daily part of their professional, educational, and personal lives.

In addition, those of us who knew, worked, and learned with Steve Stahl, colleague and friend, want to dedicate this book to his memory. No one could be more caring about the education of young children; no one could be more obtuse in his personal conversations. Steve would have laughed the loudest if he had read this dedication.

CONTENTS

FOREWORD

S everal years ago, I was honored to be asked to serve on my professional organization's research committee. A high school teacher and researcher, I joined university researchers, members of research institutes, and editors of journals to provide leadership for the research direction of the organization. I approached my first committee meeting hesitantly. An African American man seated nearby smiled, put out his hand, and introduced himself as a professor from a well-known university, adding that he was newly appointed to the committee. I introduced myself and said that I, too, was newly appointed, describing myself as a representative high school teacher. He raised an eyebrow, smiled again, and said, "We better sit together."

At the time, both K–12 teachers and African Americans were rarely members of such committees and, as a result, the two of us were often asked to speak for others presumed to be like us. Although we could speak only for ourselves, our presence changed the context in which the committee made its decisions. I had known that the context of my classroom, including my own actions and beliefs, affected the research I conducted, but I had not realized how much the colleagues in my research community also contributed. This book is a tribute to the work that colleagues, with all their differences, contribute to one another's research and learning.

The research community created by the authors of this book consists of 12 K–12 teachers and teacher educators, plus an additional teacher educator who joined in the final evaluation. They have varying amounts of experience in schools in Athens, Georgia, USA, and Champaign, Illinois, USA. They also have varying amounts of experience with research itself. They call their research design and process "critical inquiry" and devote a chapter to its origin in the thinking of Louise Rosenblatt, Paulo Freire, and Mikhail Bakhtin. They do not stop with a discussion of theory in the abstract, however. As their large cohort evolves and their research progresses, readers experience their interactions, tensions, new understandings, and growth.

Each teacher reports on his or her research, but the reports are revealed through the interactions of the small cohorts, and those interactions are analyzed as data. Teachers and their students question their own stances and opinions in a way that raises new questions. In response to the discussions recorded in this book, readers may find themselves "joining" the research group and asking questions with the authors regarding their own practices. For example, I saw the connection between my experience on the research committee and the authors' discussions of context and critical inquiry. As I thought about the issues they raised, I also asked myself the following questions:

- How do I accept responsibility for the learning in my classroom and research group?
- How do my beliefs and background intervene in my classroom teaching and research?
- How do I contribute to the learning of others, and how do they contribute to mine?

A personalized, welcoming research book such as this derives its rigor from its insistence on careful and transparent reporting of the context of the research. The authors carefully document the context of their classrooms. They also demonstrate how to raise issues of context with colleagues and describe their efforts to "flatten" the hierarchy that exists in educational research in regard to grade levels. They insist on a process of working with one another that is supportive and honest. Readers, no matter how complicated their own teaching context is, will see inquiry groups such as the ones described here as offering professional support for their growth as teachers and researchers.

There is much to learn from the classroom data that form the basis of the research in this book, although it does not emphasize "what works" in lesson plans, classroom management, or teaching methods. "What works" publications, despite their sound of certainty and finality, are inevitably revised, absorbed, and replaced through a process of experience and continued research. Readers of this book will learn about the process of continuing research as the members of this inquiry community document and analyze their experiences to produce new understandings for their students, their colleagues, and themselves. The authors have written a hopeful book of research about teaching, a book to be trusted.

Marian M. Mohr
Fairfax County Public Schools (Retired)
Fairfax County, Virginia, USA

ACKNOWLEDGMENTS

We, the 13 authors of this book, want to thank the Lyle Spencer Foundation and the International Reading Association for graciously and generously funding the grants that made this work possible. We just wish that, in the future, such grants will be unnecessary because this kind of work will be an accepted and supported norm in the work of K–12 teachers and teacher educators.

In addition, we want to thank Heidi Metrakoudas and Hellen Inyega for taking care of all the small details so we could focus on our work. Their contributions were invaluable.

ABOUT THE AUTHORS

Jennifer Aaron
Third-Grade Teacher
Clarke County Schools
Athens, Georgia, USA

Eurydice Bouchereau Bauer
Associate Professor of Language
  and Literacy
University of Illinois at Urbana–
  Champaign
Champaign, Illinois, USA

Michelle Commeyras
Professor of Reading Education
University of Georgia
Athens, Georgia, USA

Sharon Dowling Cox
Speech–Language Pathologist
Honey Creek Elementary School
Conyers, Georgia, USA

Bren Daniell
Fifth-Grade Teacher
Honey Creek Elementary School
Conyers, Georgia, USA

Ellen Elrick
Elementary Teacher
Dr. Howard School
Champaign, Illinois, USA

Bob Fecho
Associate Professor of Reading
  Education
University of Georgia
Athens, Georgia, USA

Jill Hermann-Wilmarth
Assistant Professor of Teaching,
  Learning, and Leadership
Western Michigan University
Kalamazoo, Michigan, USA

Elizabeth Hogan
English Teacher
Champaign, Illinois Unit 4 Schools
Champaign, Illinois, USA

Andrea Pintaone-Hernandez
First-Grade Teacher
Clarke County Schools
Athens, Georgia, USA

Kathy Roulston
Assistant Professor of Qualitative
  Research
University of Georgia
Athens, Georgia, USA

Amanda Siegel
Elementary Teacher
Saint Andrew's School
Saratoga, California, USA

Hope Vaughn
Secondary English Teacher
Elberton, Georgia, USA

CHAPTER 1

Of Horses, Communities, Responsibility, and Risk: Raising Our Questions

On a screened porch on a Saturday morning in midautumn of 2002, three K–12 teachers, a doctoral graduate student, and two teacher educators were in the midst of discussing the ways critical inquiry pedagogy played out in their respective classrooms. This Athens, Georgia, USA, assemblage of educators comprised two thirds of a research community that had come together as a K–university partnership; the other third of the research community resided in Champaign, Illinois, USA. Warm sunlight filtered through the just-turning leaves of the trees that shaded the house, and a slight breeze ruffled papers from time to time as the discussion wended its wandering way among us. We in the Athens branch of the research community had been talking for close to 90 minutes when Hope Vaughn, one of the teachers in our group and a sixth-grade language arts teacher, raised a point. She suggested that we all seemed to be talking about *critical inquiry* and *critical inquiry pedagogy* as if we knew what they were and we all agreed to what they meant.

There was an awkward silence for a moment. Of course, we had been assuming a shared discourse. After all, hadn't we all, in various combinations, been in graduate classes together as learners and facilitators where we had studied this issue, hadn't some of us been in independent study groups that focused on critical inquiry and critical inquiry pedagogy, and hadn't a few of us written or presented together on these ideas? Maybe so, but we sensed there was more diversity of perspective among us in this space than we'd been willing to admit, because doing so would have meant we would have had to explore those differences. Exploring is hard work. Why would we have disturbed the tenor of that lovely morning? Yet it seemed that because we are advocates for inquiry stances on classrooms that are critical, we had little choice.

Sensing the importance of this discussion, Michelle Commeyras, a teacher educator, raised a challenge:

> If we can say what critical inquiry is individually for us, and then look across us as a group, that will allow us to articulate something that might be of interest to others. We all will contribute some shades or some examples of what we have come to think of as critical inquiry.

Given this opening into the dialogue, Bob Fecho, another teacher educator, tried to position his response in terms of ideas that he had been mulling over for several years:

When inquiry becomes critical, the social, the political, and the cultural domains come into focus. I am going back and forth on this. For example, my preservice students are discovering ways that they can work with struggling readers. That might just be *plain inquiry*, from my perspective, but if then they start exploring the importance of the sociocultural and political context of readers' lives, then that moves into critical inquiry. What is the struggling readers' position in the school, and how might that be problematic? When students move into the critical realm, they are questioning what is out there and what it means. They have different understandings of that, and I am fine with that. It is the exploration and questioning of ideas and social positions of all struggling readers that I want to encourage.

As was often the case early in the history of the Athens group, comments by Michelle and Bob set the stage for ensuing discussion.

In this case, neither had long to wait, as Hope offered this comment:

Does that make critical inquiry more personal for the teacher, too? When you become more aware of what adolescent students bring to their writing, then you may become aware of their income and the things that are going on in their home. Do you as a teacher researcher become involved in that? Does it matter if you do become personally involved?

Jill Hermann-Wilmarth, a teacher educator teaching preservice education classes at the University of Georgia (UGA), picked up Hope's thread:

I think it does. I am taking what I learn about my students' life contexts into how I teach. I have to listen to who they are, and that necessarily affects who I become in the classroom. My inquiry also is about myself and how I change, as I come to know my students.

Choosing her words carefully, Bren Daniell, a fifth-grade teacher, weighed in with ideas that would carry through much of her future inquiry.

In studying my teaching practice, I find myself examining everything I do in relation to the students. I have to look at myself resisting some things, and this causes me to look at my entire life in different ways. It has been hard. Am I racist? How racist am I? Do I have prejudices? Am I slanting this because I want students to come to a certain conclusion?

And so the conversation continued, with teachers and teacher educators adding ideas, building on points made by others, and raising questions and concerns about the critical inquiry process.

The discussion eventually progressed to the idea of students and teachers self-interrogating their own stances, of not only calling into question what others believe, but also calling their own beliefs into question. Hope raised a concern about trying to shield sixth-grade students from her personal view because "it's difficult not to shape their ideas."

Michelle responded, "I hear a difference among telling students we have a perspective, telling why we have that perspective, and showing how we attempt to interrogate our own perspectives. It is far more difficult to interrogate my thinking than to explain it."

Bob followed by further reminding the group that we, as educators, "are learning critical inquiry at the same time as our students" and that "the idea of self-interrogation becomes really important" as a means for educators to reflect on their practice.

Giving consideration to what had been said earlier in the discussion about critical inquiry and critical inquiry pedagogy, Jill wondered aloud to the others:

> The egocentric issue that I have is that it becomes an all-consuming thing. Is it okay if you are consumed with reflecting on how what you are doing in your classroom affects your students? Sometimes I feel that I need to be thinking about my students more than myself.

Andrea Pintaone-Hernandez, a young teacher barely months into her first teaching job, had been sitting quietly taking in much of this conversation. However, prompted by Jill's concern, she suggested, "The more I question, the more I become less egocentric. The more I reflect, the more I lose myself in my students."

■ A Horse of a Different Color: Developing Our View of Critical Inquiry Pedagogy

This conversation took place fairly early in our incarnation as a research community. As we sat on Michelle's porch, we struggled to learn about one another, to open ourselves to a range of ideas, and to trust our group to be supportive of one another. As we in Athens tried to ferret these issues, the contingent in Champaign—Eurydice Bouchereau Bauer, Ellen Elrick, and Amanda Siegel—struggled with these and other concerns. Even as we added Sharon Dowling Cox, Jennifer Aaron, and Elizabeth Hogan in the second year of our work and asked Kathy Roulston to act as a third-party evaluator, we continued to deepen and make even more complex our sense of critical inquiry and critical inquiry pedagogy and what they meant for our classrooms.

Evident in the dialogue and many ensuing dialogues is a sense that we were nowhere near a consensus as to what we meant when we said critical inquiry. Nearly three years later, as we assembled the various pieces of this book, our views about critical inquiry pedagogy and taking such a stance in our classroom remained far ranging. Over this time, our perspectives changed, not necessarily in broad convolutions, but more commonly in a deepening and layering of views brought on by our many discussions, data-gathering excursions, presentations, and writing sessions. Our understanding of what we believed about critical inquiry pedagogy and why we believed it became much more nuanced, incisive, and connected as we transacted with these issues with purpose and across time.

We suspect there are some readers who would wonder why a group of educators dedicated to exploring critical inquiry pedagogy wouldn't have, surely after three years of focused investigation, a much greater consensus built around our definition and purposes for the term. Some of these readers might say, "What was the point of all that time and effort if not to clarify and unify your beliefs?" The short response to this concern is that our investigation into critical inquiry has helped us to understand that, for members of a research community, to dialogue on a range of issues through a range of perspectives is a preferred condition—that, by honoring multiple viewpoints in our research community, we enter into a state of grace that is neither too rigidly conceived nor too loosely construed. The resulting community remains in a healthy state of tempered flux.

Our longer response to that concern is this book, the focus of which is to document how we investigated issues of critical inquiry, the range of what we came to understand about this topic, and the possibilities such work presents to us and other educators. Our intent is for this book to be multi-voiced. By doing so, it will represent the 13 authors who collaborated—new and veteran teachers, those experienced with and those being introduced to critical inquiry, teachers of first graders and teachers of preservice teachers—and attempt to show both the range and depth of our thinking. Furthermore, we seek to show the way a community of teachers inquiring critically into practice can serve as a system of professional support through which new and veteran teachers can evolve ways of teaching that seek to engage them and their students while honoring the constraints of the various agendas and curricula of educational stakeholders.

■ A Horse With No Name: The Genesis of Our Research Community

Some readers might also wonder why a group that has opened itself to critique and discussion has no name after three years. Have we no sense of identity? Are we so loosely conjoined that we have little sense of belonging? In response, we paraphrase a story that the writer J.D. Salinger (1959/1963) used to start his novella, *Raise High the Roof Beam, Carpenters*. In this story, a Chinese duke needed a new horse and assigned the task of locating one to a respected horse trader. The horse trader, however, was unable to make the journey due to advanced age and suggested that the emperor send in his stead a good friend, who was by trade a grocer. The duke agreed and the grocer began looking for a horse befitting a man of the duke's station. After much time, the grocer sent word that he had found a dun mare that would more than satisfy the duke's needs. Delighted, the duke dispatched the asking price, and the grocer purchased and delivered the horse. Shortly thereafter, the duke confronted his horse trader in a rage. "Your grocer doesn't know what he's doing," he screamed. "He said he had a wonderful dun-colored mare for me. Yet when I went to the stables, I found a black stallion." In alarm, the horse trader went to see the new animal and, indeed, it was a black stallion. Somewhat to the dismay of the duke, a smile crossed the face of his horse trader. "How can you smile at such a gross mistake?" bellowed the duke. "There is no mistake," offered the horse trader. "It's just that my friend the grocer has gotten so good that he no longer bothers with minor details. He looks at the things he ought to look at and neglects those that need not be looked at." And it was so. The horse turned out to be the finest in the stable and most befitting the duke.

Although we in no way see ourselves as skilled in detecting that which matters most in terms of critical inquiry pedagogy as the grocer was in locating a befitting horse—we all are apprentices—we do have one trait in common with him: In our search to better understand issues of critical inquiry pedagogy, we have learned to focus our precious time on issues of substance beyond minor details. Despite having, on occasion, used meeting time to consider name possibilities and playing with acronyms that have provided us a certain amount of amusement, we have never seen a catchy name as significant or necessary enough to capture our full attention. Informally, we have always taken the name of our first benefactor—the Lyle Spencer Foundation, who funded our work with a grant specific to the needs of teacher researchers—and have referred to ourselves as the Spencer

Group, knowing full well that, due to the philanthropy of that foundation, any number of Spencer groups might exist at any given time at various places in the world.

Eurydice, Michelle, and Bob originally conceived the idea for the research community now composed of two cohorts in Athens and one cohort in Champaign. When Bob arrived at UGA having recently left his high school teaching position in a close-knit, small learning community, he had been looking for colleagues with whom to share discussions of pedagogy. Michelle and Eurydice, fueled by their work with undergraduates, were equally interested in having such discussions, and so a collaboration was born in which they each conducted practitioner research on their university undergraduate classrooms (Fecho, Commeyras, Bauer, & Font, 2000). Gratified by the success of that early collaboration that focused on issues of authority in critical inquiry classrooms and concerned by the ways young teachers interested in inquiry pedagogy frequently felt unsupported in their attempts to enact such inquiry, Eurydice, Michelle, and Bob began to imagine an inquiry community that would not only help them continue their work but also widen the range of professional support.

The original design of the project was predicated upon a few governing principles:

1. The structure of the project would be a nested one in which we would form three cohorts consisting of one teacher educator and two former students of that teacher educator, with a third former student being added to each cohort in the second year of the project. Each cohort would meet regularly on their own as well as periodically as a large research community consisting of all three cohorts. Generally, we referred to the groups of four educators as the *small cohorts* and to the whole research community as the *large cohort*.

2. The cohorts would be formed with as much of an eye for diversity— age, race, ethnicity, sexual identity, gender, years teaching—as their relatively small numbers can accommodate.

3. Although the teacher educators would serve as research mentors to the less research-experienced K–12 teachers, all classrooms were open to mutual research, and data gathered by the team there would be shared within and among the small cohorts. As much as possible, traditional hierarchies present in university–school partnerships— hierarchies that tend to privilege the university personnel—would be

flattened, and the K–12 teachers would be encouraged to take leadership roles and responsibilities.

4. The focus of the work would be inquiry pedagogy in general and critical inquiry pedagogy in particular, with each individual researcher and each cohort developing subquestions under those umbrellas.

The intent behind these four principles would be to create a research community in which teachers and teacher educators could share a range of teaching, learning, research, and leadership roles as necessary and consider concerns of critical inquiry pedagogy from a range of perspectives. We also hoped that, as teacher educators working with our former education students, the small and large cohorts would come up to speed faster because academic and personal relationships already had been formed.

In action, we have tried to adhere to these principles as the project evolved, although we've needed to take some variance at times. For example, when Eurydice, who had been a colleague of Bob's and Michelle's at UGA, accepted a job at the University of Illinois, just as Michelle and Bob were forming their cohorts in Athens, it became obvious that Eurydice's cohort in Champaign—now some 500 miles away from Athens—could not consist of former students, nor would our large cohort be able to meet as frequently as originally imagined, due to the distance. Although such variances complicated our ways of working, they also opened us to possibilities, which, sadly, were not always acted on (see chapter 6), but helped or had the potential to help us enrich our experience.

■ Looking a Gift Horse in the Mouth: Identifying the Cohort Members

We firmly believe that we are what we investigate. Our choices for what we inquire about and the means with which we inquire reflect our identities and the ways we see the world. In keeping with this belief, we will, at the beginning of chapters 3 through 5, use the Stories of Our Questions—in which the authors of each chapter discuss the background of how and why certain classroom issues became important to them—to more thoroughly connect each of us to these individual cohort chapters. We feel these explanations of our questions and how we were attracted to them provide insight into what we considered valuable, at least at the onset of our investigations, in terms of understanding our classrooms. Although our questions evolved over time, these glimpses into where we began our work are the genesis of a description of individual and collective transformation that this book continues to flesh out. Furthermore, the Stories of Our Questions help to position us as individuals within the large cohort.

Still, with a cast of characters as large as we present here, readers will need to grasp some sense of who we are. The narrative that opens this chapter hints at both the diversity and the commonality we brought to this project. The many voices, personalities, experiences, and perspectives we hope will provide rich dialogue, but we are concerned that they also will create a certain amount of confusion regarding who is saying what to whom. Having already started introducing ourselves via the narrative, we want to continue the process—one that will extend through the book.

Gathering the Small Cohorts

Although the original intent of the grant from the Lyle Spencer Foundation was to have Michelle, Eurydice, and Bob work with their previous students on the inquiry project, Eurydice could not accomplish this goal given her new employment at the University of Illinois. To proceed with the grant, she asked Ellen, her daughter's teacher, in the fall of 2001 to join the project. She then asked the principal of Ellen's school to identify another teacher who might be open to examining their teaching in a small, supportive cohort. She suggested that Eurydice approach Amanda, who agreed to join them, and thus their initial small cohort was formed. Because teachers in their small cohort were relative novices to teaching, they discussed adding an experienced teacher in the second year of the grant. Eurydice asked a colleague for names of experienced teachers, and her colleague recommended Elizabeth, a high school teacher. Adding Elizabeth to the group had unintended results. Ellen and Amanda saw Elizabeth's National Board Certification status as something they might want to strive for in the future. Although their cohort was constructed differently from the Athens cohorts, they believed their configuration offered a glimpse into what teachers are capable of accomplishing even without the benefit of knowing one another prior to a project.

Bob, in thinking about whom he wanted to work with, saw the task of selecting cohorts as a no-brainer. At the time, Andrea was pursuing her master's degree, and Bob was her thesis chair. Knowing how well she embraced the theory of critical inquiry pedagogy, how she had been actively involved in an independent study group he led on narrative inquiry, and how she brought care to working with young children, Andrea seemed to be a perfect choice. Hope also stood out to Bob when she was a member of his secondary reading class as a preservice teacher. Impressed by her insight into cultural issues impacting adolescents and her willingness to reflect on her own practice, Bob immediately thought of Hope as a complement to Andrea and himself. Moving into the second year of the study, the small cohort saw Jennifer as a natural fit. Her interest in upper-grades elementary students doing academic service learning, a form of inquiry pedagogy that involved students in the community and the community with students, and her intent to include them in her dissertation research allowed her to smoothly integrate her style and ideas into an already functioning small cohort.

In organizing her small cohort—the second one in Athens—Michelle asked Bren and Jill to join her because they both had just completed Michelle's seminar on sociopolitical perspectives in literacy education. Because Jill did a project in Bren's classroom that was related to literature and critical inquiry, Michelle thought they would work well together. In particular, Michelle admired both of them as writers, which means that she also found that they were good analytic thinkers and facile at the kind of give-and-take that would be important in discussing their goals as teachers. When it came time to adding a fourth person to their cohort, Michelle, Bren, and Jill agreed that they wanted to ask Sharon, who taught in the same school as Bren and also had been in Michelle's literacy and sociopolitical issues seminar. Given the discussion of race that already was part of their critical inquiry, they wanted to get Sharon's African American perspective on issues. In the end, the bottom line for Michelle was that all three teachers were hardworking, had inquiring minds, and were fun to be with.

Self-Identification Descriptors

Looking at how those of us in the large cohort self-identify, we are somewhat of an abstract mosaic, multicolored tiles adding up to a composite more impressionistically than definitively whole. A viewer senses tones and possibilities rather than a stark portraiture. In an attempt to help readers gain some facile and more distinct sense of our large cohort's range of diversity and commonality, we have provided a table of self-descriptors organized by cohort (see Table 1). We view self-identity under these categories—gender; race, ethnicity, or both; sexual identity; years of education experience; and teaching assignments—as important because of how these descriptions self-resonate with many of the themes and issues of this book. In addition to these agreed-upon categories, we have included an "open" self-identification category. Therefore, if a group member saw religion or being a parent as an important way to self-identify in terms of our teaching, he or she might

Table 1
Spencer Group Self-Identification Descriptors

Community Cohort	Gender	Race or Ethnicity, or Both	Sexual Identity	Years of Education Experience as of 2004	Teaching Assignments	Other Information Deemed Pertinent by the Author
Elizabeth Hogan	Female	Irish American	Hetero-sexual	9	Secondary English, writing, and literature	Lesbian and gay ally
Amanda Siegel	Female	Caucasian	Hetero-sexual	2	Third, fourth, and fifth grades	
Eurydice Bouchereau Bauer	Female	Haitian American	Hetero-sexual	18	University teacher educator	Raised biculturally, mother of two bicultural and bilingual children, strongly committed to cultural and linguistic diversity
Ellen Elrick	Female	Caucasian	Hetero-sexual	4	Second grade	

Responsibility Cohort	Gender	Race or Ethnicity, or Both	Sexual Identity	Years of Education Experience as of 2004	Teaching Assignments	Other Information Deemed Pertinent by the Author
Bob Fecho	Male	Eastern European American	Hetero-sexual	30	Teacher educator in language and literacy education	Raised working class, father of daughters, husband
Hope Vaughn	Female	Caucasian of German, Cherokee, and Irish heritage	Hetero-sexual	3	Middle and high school	Christian, dweller in the rural southern United States, mother
Andrea Pintaone-Hernandez	Female	Caucasian	Hetero-sexual	3	Head Start, first and second grades	
Jennifer Aaron	Female	Caucasian	Hetero-sexual	7	Third and fifth grades	

(continued)

Table 1 (continued)
Spencer Group Self-Identification Descriptors

Risk Cohort	Gender	Race or Ethnicity, or Both	Sexual Identity	Years of Education Experience as of 2004	Teaching Assignments	Other Information Deemed Pertinent by the Author
Bren Daniell	Female	White		27	Fifth grade	
Sharon Dowling Cox	Female	African American		22	Speech–language pathologist	Seventh daughter, child advocate
Jill Hermann-Wilmarth	Female	White	Lesbian	7	University teacher educator	
Michelle Commeyras	Female	White, born in France but an American citizen	Equal-opportunity lover	18	University teacher educator	Daughter, sister, Africanist, global citizen

include that designation in this descriptor. However, we also agreed that if one of the large cohort members felt it important, for her or his own reasons, to not respond to a category, then he or she could leave that box blank.

Despite our efforts to open up Table 1, to infuse it with some life, it remains woefully inadequate. After all, it is just a table, and no such gridding in such terse terms could serve to truly introduce the complex personas behind those descriptions. Still, we offer it for what it is, our cod-liver oil (something distasteful to swallow, but ultimately thought to be good for a person's general well-being), so to speak. In our online conversations, we discussed the need for this table and, although none of us were totally happy with it, we recognized its expediency. Given that, the dialogue and narratives of our research and research processes are the most significant means for filling in the spaces left by the table.

We also recognize that descriptors denoting racial or ethnic heritage are always in flux, being subject, like all language, to many contextual, personal, and social factors. When describing student populations and other groups in general, we have tried to consistently use the terms African American, Asian American, European American, Latino or Latina, and

Native American, wherever those terms might apply. However, when individuals in the book self-identified themselves, we kept whatever designations they were most comfortable using to describe themselves. Regardless of which terms we used, we understand that some readers might find one or another term inappropriate, but we hope that these readers will recognize that our use of these terms was our best-faith effort to acknowledge heritage in a respectful manner.

■ Horsing Around a Definition: Defining Our Terms

We have used the terms *critical inquiry* and *critical inquiry pedagogy* fairly loosely thus far, acting as if readers have a common definition for those terms and using them somewhat interchangeably. In addition, we've already noted that we don't completely agree on the specifics of those terms, although our ideas do fall into a range that can be sketched. It's one of our intentions to, in more explicit terms, describe and discuss that range, but at least as a starting point, we'll try here to explain what we mean when we use the term *critical inquiry* and how we see that term relating to *critical inquiry pedagogy*.

For us, *inquiry* is the umbrella term, one that designates a range of ways for students and teachers to explore and investigate the world around them. When an inquiry becomes *critical*, in the broadest sense, it allows students and teachers to make their own meanings of the world and to consider themselves and their identities in relationship to larger social, political, cultural, and historical factors around them. For many of us, the work of Paulo Freire (1970/1993) served as our entry into this perspective. However, the writings of others, such as Mikhail M. Bakhtin (1981), Lisa D. Delpit (1995), John Dewey (1938), bell hooks (1994), Judith W. Lindfors (1999), Louise M. Rosenblatt (1938/1995), and Ira Shor (1992), have either introduced or further provoked some or all of us to seek deeper understandings of what it means to inquire in more critical ways. It is upon this work and this barest definition that the dialogue contained in the rest of this book is built.

As the rest of this book will illuminate, critical inquiry and critical inquiry pedagogy have, for the most part, become synonymous for us. Although we can imagine instances where one could enact a critical inquiry that was outside one's pedagogy, we find it extremely difficult to separate why, what, and how we choose to explore in the world around us from why, what, and how we elect to teach in our classrooms. If we are critically inquiring, we are more than likely to be considering what such inquiry means for our teaching. If our students and us, K–university learners and educators, are critically inquiring, then we are considering what such inquiry means not only for our classrooms, but also for each of us as individuals. Therefore, we have come to see critical inquiry and critical inquiry pedagogy as terms that overlap so dramatically as to, in most cases, make the delineation moot. As such, we will more often use what we consider to be the umbrella term—*critical inquiry*—referring to *critical inquiry pedagogy* only when feeling a need to emphasize the teaching connection.

■ Making Horse Sense of the Book: Explaining Our Directions, Our Intentions, and This Book's Title

The phrase that once appeared on many beverage bottles in the United States—"no deposit, no return"—may, at first, seem an odd title for a book on critical inquiry and the impact of literacy on our lives and learning. In that context, the beverage companies, sometime after the Beatles but before Madonna, were touting that these new bottles required no up-front deposit because they could be thrown away rather than returned. Those of us old enough to remember this know that, prior to this arrangement, U.S. grocery stores and gas stations kept empty bottle cases handy to be filled by people returning bottles, and enterprising children could make lunch money by scouring back alleys and trash cans for empty bottles and returning them for a nickel deposit. However, this all changed when throwaways and recyclables came into vogue, and the cost of a deposit no longer needed to be added to the price of a beverage.

However, in our context, the idea of *"no deposit, no return"* takes on a somewhat different meaning. Our worry is that, in too many public schools today, society is making "no deposit" in the name of children learning there, so, subsequently, we in society are gaining "no return" on our collective investment. We worry that, by expecting more from teachers and students, but providing them with inadequate resources, funding, and faith in their abilities, public education will become a place where creativity, leadership, and critical thought go to die, if they haven't already. We offer this book—an example of collaborative practitioner research—as one antidote to such a fate.

Even a casual reader of teacher and practitioner research might think that there are enough book-length examples of teachers researching their classrooms (e.g., Ballenger, 1999; Fecho, 2004; Gallas, 2003; Hankins,

2003; Michie, 1999), enough vibrant anthologies dedicated to teacher and practitioner research (e.g., Allen, 1999; Graham, Hudson-Ross, Adkins, McWhorter, & Stewart, 1999; Mohr et al., 2004), and enough comprehensive and specialized reviews of the teacher and practitioner research literature (e.g., Baumann, Bisplinghoff, & Allen, 1997; Cochran-Smith & Lytle, 1999; Fecho & Allen, 2002, 2003; Fecho, Allen, Mazaros, & Inyega, 2006; Hollingsworth & Sockett, 1994; Lytle, 2000) to verify that teachers are capable of adding not only to their own individual knowledge base but also to the knowledge base of education in general. One would think that this rich body of literature speaks eloquently for itself.

However, we also recognize that to many teachers and academics, teacher and practitioner research remains somewhat of a curiosity, a practice of a small but committed group of educators whose work seems not to be fully embraced by either teachers or academics. Therefore, one purpose of this book is to demonstrate the ways K–12/university practitioner–research partnerships might provide bridges for teacher researchers into both the academic and teaching communities. Our second purpose, building upon the first, is to describe and analyze the ways in which we worked as teachers and teacher educators, as new and veteran teachers, across cultural boundaries and over time and life changes. Just as our classrooms were places where issues of community, responsibility, and risk were raised by educators and students so, too, the large cohort was a place where our cohort members raised the similar issues. That which we inquired into, we lived out in our cohorts as well. With that in mind, this book offers frameworks to teachers and teacher educators that will enable them to provide ongoing pedagogical and research support for one another. We particularly want to focus on how our work supported new and veteran teachers, thus enlarging the more narrow conceptions of what mentor–apprentice and K–12/university relationships might look like.

Our final purpose is to present an interconnected body of research that shows the complex ways critical inquiry classrooms operate, the issues that evolve in such classrooms, and the possibilities for substantive intellectual work they provide. Three themes that resonate throughout this book are that of (1) developing community, (2) assuming responsibility, and (3) taking risk. Our research—conducted in elementary, secondary, and university undergraduate classrooms—unpacks those themes in terms of critical inquiry pedagogy. The ultimate purpose is to reinvigorate a dialogue around these themes, to help all of us imagine classrooms where teachers and students transact with community, responsibility, and risk in productive ways.

In order to accomplish these three purposes, the ensuing chapters will develop these themes in a variety of ways. Chapter 2 provides a general discussion of our research methods and the underlying theories that we seek to place into action within our classrooms. In it, we argue for the value of works such as those of Louise Rosenblatt, Paulo Freire, and Mikhail Bakhtin in creating a framework for taking an inquiry stance in ways that were vital to helping us reflect on and implement critical inquiry in our classrooms.

Chapters 3, 4, and 5 describe the research the small cohorts conducted and focus on the themes of community, responsibility, and risk taking, in that order. As previously mentioned, at the beginning of each of these chapters, we've provided a section entitled the Stories of Our Questions. These short sections serve to introduce the members of each cohort through the situations in their classrooms and professional lives that were causing them to raise questions and consider ways to inquire. Our hope is that these brief descriptions will give readers a clearer sense of the individuals in each small cohort and the ways their questions brought them together.

In chapter 3, Amanda, Elizabeth, Ellen, and Eurydice investigate the ways their attempts to create communities of inquirers in their separate classrooms intersected with their mutual development as an inquiry community. In particular, they note that community is not necessarily a place where everyone agrees but instead is a place that has structures and means for evoking a range of perspectives.

Andrea, Bob, Hope, and Jennifer show in chapter 4 the way that teachers and students in a range of classroom settings were able to take responsibility for the learning that was occurring there. Specifically, they raise the argument that enabling teachers and students to take such responsibility is more useful and supportive in terms of creating substantive educational opportunities than more punitive actions, such as retaining in the same grade students who have passed course work but failed a statewide end-of-course exam.

In chapter 5, Bren, Jill, Michelle, and Sharon investigate issues of risk and what risk taking means for teachers enacting critical inquiry. They document ways in which each of them took risks in their classroom, and they raise questions as to the nature of risk. Specifically, they suggest that seeing risk as calculated and necessary for classrooms enables them to inquire about topics that are critical to understanding one's stance in relation to the rest of society.

Chapter 6 was written by Kathryn, the evaluator we hired, as previously mentioned, to give us an outsider's perspective on the ways we worked and how well we used our principles to guide our work. In that chapter, she provides an outsider's perspective into the complexity of the work of the cohorts, seeking all the while to answer the basic ethnographic question: What's going on here? Using the themes of community, responsibility, and risk, Kathryn discusses tensions and negotiations that marked the work of the group.

Chapter 7 is based upon a dialogue among all three cohorts about what this work has come to mean to us and where we see it taking us, as well as the larger educational community. In particular, we acknowledge and discuss the importance of seeing critical inquiry as a process; the complex relationship between access to power and the roles played in research communities and classrooms; the balance and play of a range of tensions among group members; and the myriad ways the themes of creating community, taking responsibility, and exploring risk transacted within our cohorts. At the close of the book, we offer a formal breakdown of cohort participants and their teaching positions and affiliations in Appendix A, while providing a specific glimpse into the focus and methods of each cohort member's study in Appendix B.

■ One More Horse Tale: The Importance of Our Collaboration

Very little in our research community comes easily or without a good deal of discussion. When our group tried to flatten hierarchies, we opened ourselves to complexity that has affected us in many ways. For example, we try, whenever making important decisions that affect the group, to consider the needs, voices, and divergent perspectives of all the members. And we think we've gotten better at this over time. Although this consideration often slows down our processes and, at times, creates overanalysis of some issues, we would rather err on the side of dialogue than efficiency—but perhaps we should have opened that point to the group as well.

When it came to deciding the line of authorship for this book, we arrived at an almost immediate consensus that all 13 of us would be listed as authors. We had, after all, written the book in various individual and collective ways. However, order became another issue. In the academic community, position on a byline indicates the relative contribution to the work by each author, with the first author having taken greatest responsibility for the work and the last author the least. Very often, judgments about promotion and tenure are made based upon such placement. Still, to establish some sort of hierarchy of a not easily quantified effort seemed to go against the principles upon which the group was founded.

Our discussion via e-mail eventually yielded four possibilities to decide the order of authorship: (1) strict alphabetical order, (2) alphabetical order with the three of us who started the project first, (3) alphabetical order with all university authors first, or (4) random order. Using a form of consensus voting, we decided that, for the sake of supporting our efforts to share both honor and responsibility, we would go by strict alphabetical order.

When Salinger ended the tale of the horse trader, he had the narrator, Buddy Glass, indicate that his brother, Seymour, like the old grocer in the story, was the only person he would send looking for horses in his stead. For our large cohort, although each one of us would trust the other to purchase horses in our stead, perhaps a more remarkable idea has taken root. We have come to realize, though it might be a slow and difficult process, in the end, it would be better to send all of us on the trail of prime horseflesh.

CHAPTER 2

Talking With Louise, Paulo, and Mikhail: Connecting to the Work of Rosenblatt, Freire, and Bakhtin

lthough Louise Rosenblatt, Paulo Freire, and Mikhail Bakhtin weren't physically present on Michelle Commeyras's porch that fall morning described in chapter 1, these three theorists—or at least their ideas— managed to have a voice in that and many conversations to follow. Rarely mentioned by name, Rosenblatt, Freire, and Bakhtin sat in the corners, looked over our shoulders, listened in on our conversations, and nodded or shook their heads accordingly. Somewhat like the picture of the father in *The Glass Menagerie* (Williams, 1945), a man who fell in love with long distances and whose presence literally and figuratively hung over the lives of the rest of the family, the work of Rosenblatt, Freire, and Bakhtin informed and was made evident in our own work.

This chapter traces the ways in which the ideas of Rosenblatt, Freire, and Bakhtin—or Louise, Paulo, and Mikhail, as we like to call them—served as a framework from which we built our various inquiries. Our worry, however, is that at the mere mention of theory, we'll lose half of our readers, some of whom will vault over this chapter and merrily proceed through the rest of the book; we also worry that this chapter will serve as a terminus for other readers, those who are too disenchanted with theory to go on. For many teachers, *theory* has become an alien word, something they associate with courses they took in college that seem to have no near nor remote connection to the everyday concerns of their classrooms. "Oh, that's just an Aderhold thing" is a phrase often repeated in faculty lunchrooms in northern Georgia schools. It refers to the main building that houses the University of Georgia College of Education, Athens, Georgia, USA. This phrase is used by some area teachers to dismiss an approach or activity as being too idealistic or theoretical to possibly be of use in a working classroom. Yet, as our cohort has come to understand, there is no practice without theory, and taking steps to identify and make theory operational creates classrooms and inquiry communities where, frankly, all stakeholders get more bang for their buck.

Accordingly, we'll focus this chapter through two lenses. First, we will argue for the necessity of theory and practice to overtly transact in the lives of all teachers and teacher educators. Second, we will unpack the work of Rosenblatt, Freire, and Bakhtin to provide a clearer sense of the overt and tacit ways their theory informed our classroom inquiries and our ways of working as an inquiry community. Specifically, we want to show how this theory helped us to first imagine and then realize our inquiry community, how the theory and the practice were intimately bound together. Ultimately, our intent is not to force our theoretical perspectives on the reader, but rather to encourage all readers to engage in their own conversations with theory and practice.

■ Theory and *Jerry Maguire*: Discussing Theory Among Teachers, Educators, and Policymakers

At some point in the history of the English language, the noun *theory* and its verb form *theorize* seemed to become separated from the everyday world of most working people and somehow became the sole possession of academics. Somewhere along the line, *theorize* became what scientists and philosophers did but not what bank tellers, assembly line workers, corporate managers, or insurance sales workers did. And if any of the latter actually did theorize, they told no one because to do so usually wasn't valued in their culture. We're reminded of the opening scenes of the movie *Jerry Maguire* (Brooks, Crowe, Mark, & Sakai, 1996), during which the title character prints and distributes to his company his theory of what it takes to run an ethical sports agency. Greeted by applause for his courage, Jerry Maguire soon finds himself out of work as his coworkers and bosses conspire to excise what they see as at least an unsightly blemish, if not a full-blown cancer, on the skin of their corporate conformity. By offering a theory, Jerry became, in the eyes of his company, two things not to be trusted: (1) a thinker and (2) an individual.

Yet, even if we don't call it that or recognize its impact in our lives, theory is what we create, and theorize is what we do, most likely daily—all of us, to a person. We make theories about the weather, why our bus is late, how to win the lottery, why men or women act as they do, what counts in life, and on and on. Jerry Maguire's coworkers, even as they branded him an outsider for his theories and theorizing, were working off and concocting new theories about themselves, their work, and their conception of Jerry. Yet, despite this omnipresence of theory, too many people too frequently surrender such work to an elite few, thereby giving away freely some of their own power.

Perhaps nowhere is this gap between the world of academia and the rest of the working world truer than in the rift that seems to exist around theory between K–12 teachers and teacher educators. The latter have been stereotyped as elitists living in their ivied halls having no sense of the reality of elementary, middle school, and high school classrooms. For their part, K–12 teachers get pegged as being anti-intellectuals who mindlessly but effectively resist educational change by merely doing nothing, and the system becomes mired in their inertia. The separation between K–12 teachers and teacher educators has been so complete that it is not uncommon to hear K–12 teachers say something akin to "I don't believe in theory," which always leaves us wondering if the speakers grasp the irony that to posit a disbelief in theory is, in fact, to theorize. On the other hand, we can hardly blame teachers for being resistant to theory considering the plethora of theories that universities produce, their short shelf life, and the lack of dialogue across those theories.

We believe it is in the complex gray areas between these stereotypes and stances where the real possibility for theoretical dialogue exists. In particular, we don't want to posit an image of teacher educators being all theoretical nor an image of teachers being completely antitheoretical. Still, the teacher educators in our group concede that they have more, and perhaps too much, time to think. Conversely, our K–12 teachers agree that they often do not have enough time to think. There's something wrong with both of these situations: The former can lead to ideas that may have little grounding in reality, and the latter can lead to too great a reliance on instinct or routine. Certainly people who work as teacher educators at universities need to spend more time in their community and schools. However, it also is our belief that people who work as K–12 teachers need to be in dialogue with those at the university.

The two traits that Jerry Maguire's coworkers feared in Jerry—being a thinker and an individual—are the two traits this inquiry community wants to see more evident in teachers and teacher educators. We worry that current federal, state, and local educational policies are taking individualism and thinking out of schools. It's bad enough that students are expected to conform to one set of values and one narrow approach to learning, but more constrictions—for example, state-mandated testing—are being placed upon teachers and teacher educators as well. The two stakeholders that seem to have the greatest investment in teaching and learning—students and teachers—seem to be the ones with the least say in the process. At the same time, the work of most teacher educators—the ones entrusted with educating future teachers—too often is marginalized by policymakers and the public in general.

We believe mucking with theory helps the individual realize the power they wield within the larger society. As we will discuss shortly, the work of three theorists—Rosenblatt, Freire, and Bakhtin—resonates strongly across the work of the large cohort. However, these ideas, because they have been filtered through our individual experiences, are interpreted somewhat differently by all of us. What Jill Hermann-Wilmarth—an out-lesbian teacher educator in Athens, Georgia, with a few years' teaching experience—makes of the work of these theorists is perceptibly different from the perspective of Ellen Elrick—a fairly new teacher in Champaign, Illinois, in a heterosexual relationship. The ongoing dialogue about these ideas by Jill, Ellen, and the rest of the large cohort creates an experience through self- and other-interrogation that helps us to keep our theories stable yet in play. At the same time, our large cohort also is shaping us as we reshape it in the process.

It is our belief that reconnecting teachers and teacher educators to a mutual dialogue around issues of theory and practice will enable thinking individuals to be taken off the endangered species list of our public schools. The intent is to bring dialogue to educational spaces where currently little or no dialogue exists. However, our intent is not to create a form of raging relativism, or schools where anything goes. Instead, our hope is to use the intersection of theory and practice to create a range of possibility for classrooms as well as for teacher education. The intent is not to shut out the policymakers—even though too many of them currently seem intent on shutting out local or dissenting voices—but instead to enter into dialogue with policymakers to fully realize what we hope was a well-intended, but a badly implemented, idea—educationally leaving no child behind.

■ Theories That Sang to Us: Unpacking Rosenblatt, Freire, and Bakhtin

Some members of our large cohort find it hard to believe that anyone can resist the siren call of complex and invigorating educational theory. Yet other members, at least as our group formed, were all too willing to do as the sailors under the command of Ulysses did—plug their ears with wax so as to not crash on the rocks of theory. As we wrote this book, all of us had become more aware of those theories that drive us individually and as a group, with some of us more avidly embracing some theories over others. Ultimately though, the transactional theories of Rosenblatt (1994, 1938/1995), the praxis theories of Freire (1970/1993), and the dialogic theories of Bakhtin (1981) sing most consistently and powerfully to all of us.

As Michelle, Eurydice Bouchereau Bauer, and Bob Fecho conjured up visions of this inquiry community, it was their aim to create a transactional space (Rosenblatt 1938/1995, 1994) where theory and practice—thought and action—would remain in dialogue (Freire, 1970/1993). In this space, a unified conception of the *inquiry community* would act in centripetal ways to stabilize and shape the community even as multiple perspectives provided centrifugal tensions to keep the community in an ongoing generative process (Bakhtin, 1981). How this conception played out will be the stuff of the rest of this book, but for the moment, the discussion will center on unpacking this conception to develop a better sense of these individual ideas. Although it is now very difficult for us to separate one theorist from the others, for the sake of comprehension we will discuss each theorist separately before discussing them as a group at the end of the chapter. Our discussion of the work of the theorists in this section will focus on one reference from each theorist. For the sake of readability, after an original citing of the source material, we'll refrain from citing each time.

Talking With Louise Rosenblatt: Unpacking Transactional Theory

When considering the concept of *transactions*, most people immediately think of financial transactions, of money changing hands for goods or services that they purchased. We're certain that this common idea of transaction is not what Rosenblatt (1938/1995) envisions in *Literature as Exploration*, and we think other metaphors and descriptions might be more useful and illuminating. For us, a transaction is much more complex than a mere giving and receiving. Instead we feel the term describes activity where readers consider context, both temporal and spatial, and those persons and/or objects involved shape one another in ways that create new "texts" that are based upon the original texts.

What does that definition mean? Rosenblatt asserts that she built upon the ideas of Dewey and Bentley (1949) and Peirce (1931–1958) and offers a means of developing a response to literature that brought the reader into the interpretive equation, a perspective Richards (1929/1950) and other New Critics, members of a predominant literary movement that argues for the primacy of text in terms of meaning making, deny. She expresses her belief that we read efferently, or for information, but that we also read aesthetically, for emotional response. Although schools have long privileged informational reading over trying to help students sort out emotions on a given text, Rosenblatt argues that readers really can't do one without the other, that we're always reading, to some degree of each, both efferently and aesthetically.

When we read for information and emotional response, we are transacting, or some educators might say dialoguing, with the text and, as we see it, creating new texts. Because each of us reads any text by bringing all our experience to that text, all readers bring personal interpretations to all texts. These interpretations may intersect with the interpretations of others, or they may differ markedly. As Rosenblatt states, "There are no generic readers or generic interpretations but only innumerable relationships between readers and texts" (1938/1995, p. 291). Connecting to our earlier discussion, Jill, because her experiences have been different from Ellen's, has potential for interpretations that Ellen might not make, and, of course, the reverse is true. In addition, because Jill and Ellen are experiencing text, they, too, become new texts. What we mean here is that the reader not only shapes the text, but the text shapes the reader, changing us to varying degrees in the process. Therefore, when they transact with a new text, their responses might differ based upon their most recent transaction. And so the process continues with each new transaction, generating new texts in ways that "recogniz[e] the dynamic to and fro relationship" (p. 292) between text and reader.

Falling back on a metaphor, Bob (Fecho, 2004) once described *transaction* as a card game in which each play is predicated upon what has come before, and all players differently read the various texts of the game. Perhaps another useful image might be that of a kaleidoscope. Each turn of the lens causes the colored glass to reform, but each new incarnation springs forth from the ones that came before, no matter how random the result may appear. The pieces of glass line up in any given way because the previous arrangement to some extent facilitated the current one. In this way, past context and the current arrangement give way to new contexts and arrangements, but all are linked in the ongoing process with each new arrangement open to multiple interpretations.

Although Rosenblatt was primarily interested in transactions between readers and printed text, she conceded that humans constantly are transacting with their environment. Freire (1983) describes such transactions as "reading the world and the word" (p. 17), and the New London Group (2000) argues for wider definitions of what counts as text and how we read such texts. In this broader sense, we "read" everything around us and are in a constant process of transaction, much of which tacitly happens. A computer-generated graphic splashed online, the sweet-tart smell of apples baking in crust, the heat shimmer rising from a desert highway, the sonorous voice of a cello being played in a practice room as you pass by are all capable of being read and are texts ripe for transaction.

Michelle, Eurydice, and Bob embraced the concept of *transaction* at its most narrow and most wide junctures. What, they wondered, would it mean if a community of K–12 teachers and teacher educators read the educational literature on critical inquiry and discussed what enticed and concerned them in that literature? Furthermore, what if they saw their classrooms as texts on critical inquiry, texts to be explored, considered, and responded to? If we brought a range of interpretations to those texts, if we all transacted with them and shared our transactions, what would we come to know? Rather than having so many of our transactions occur beneath our consciousness, what would happen if we raised them to the consciousness and interrogated them as a group? The possibilities were tantalizing, and as we looked for means to think critically about our own teaching transactions, we turned to the work of Freire.

Talking With Paulo Freire: Unpacking Praxis

One of the difficulties our cohort confronted was trying to come to a common vocabulary and avoiding unnecessary jargon. Freire's (1970/1993) concept of *praxis*, as set forth in his *Pedagogy of the Oppressed*, was a new term for some members of the cohort but was a useful one nonetheless; it gave us a name for that transactional space where theory intersects with practice. In Freirian terms, *praxis* characterizes the ongoing relationship between thought and action. We see the connection between praxis and transaction: Both are continuing processes that have historical contexts and yield new thinking and, in terms of praxis, new action. Furthermore, just as the reader and the text in a transaction are in an ongoing, recursive relationship, Freire argues that "action and reflection occur simultaneously" (p. 123) and cannot be divided into "a prior stage of reflection and a subsequent stage of action" (p. 123). To reflect is to act.

Freire built his work from his experiences teaching oppressed people in the slums of Brazil. Having seen how those in power had used education, or the lack thereof, to limit the potential of so many children and adults living in poverty, Freire developed a theory of education that was liberatory, which provided learners with ways to chart their own destinies rather than recreating roles of subjugation. Eschewing the "banking model" of teaching, where teachers fill the empty heads of students with regular deposits of information meant to prolong the status quo, Freire sought to teach literacy in ways that helped the oppressed imagine new roles for themselves and their oppressors. The idea was to liberate both the oppressed and the oppressor, to interrupt the age-old cycles and imagine new relationships.

At the heart of Freire's work is the idea of *praxis*. In particular, the thought involved in praxis is critical thought, the kind of thought that calls political, ideological, and philosophical stances into question. To get beyond the banking model, teachers and learners must enter into dialogue, calling the world as they know it into question. More important, the critical thought in praxis is reflective and introspective. As one calls the greater society into question, one also has to call one's own stances into question. It is what our cohort has come to call self- and other-interrogation.

But for Freire, critical thought was not enough. Such thought must be coupled to action. It does us little good to bring critique to our lives if we find no way to act on that critique. To think without acting and to act without thinking are the undesirable endpoints of a continuum that, akin to Rosenblatt's concept of efferent and aesthetic reading, requires we do both together.

Still, such work can be difficult and even threatening (Fecho, 2004; Fecho, Commeyras, Bauer, & Font, 2000). Too frequently, oppressors are reluctant or even hostile toward attempts to call their actions and beliefs into question. Even those open to such interrogation can find the realities of their situations difficult to accept. Freire and Macedo (1996) argue that we can't wait for all parties involved to be comfortable before embarking on these explorations, least of all ourselves. Instead, we must push learners past their zones of comfort into what Pratt (1991) has called contact zones, places where cultures transact in ways that bring power issues to the surface. It is in these uncomfortable places where, if we couple with experienced others, we can once again become independent learners (Vygotsky, 1934/1978).

The idea of praxis underlies most of our thinking and action in our inquiry community; it is played out in many ways. As we noted in chapter 1, critical inquiry springs from Freirian roots. We all sought to teach in classrooms where all perspectives, including our own, were called into question. We not only wanted to contemplate what occurred in those classrooms, but to then act on that information in ways that fostered positive change.

But the concept of praxis also helped us to shape our collaboration. As Kathy Roulston explains in chapter 6, we sought to flatten the hierarchies that exist between K–12 teachers and teacher educators, to call upon everyone's expertise and place us all into unfamiliar positions. Although we recognized the roles many university researchers had played in terms of popularizing teacher research, we worried that teacher educators mostly only mentored teachers in inquiry processes, rarely looked at their own classrooms, and almost never invited K–12 teachers to look at their classroom with them. If our experience had raised questions about these relationships, we needed to act in ways that substantively rethought and reenacted those relationships.

Perhaps most important, the concept of praxis helped us to configure our ongoing relationship to theory. If educators view theory as thought and practice as action, they can envision a new relationship between the theory and practice. The driving force behind teaching and learning is neither theory nor practice but the ongoing transaction between the two. Theory shapes practice as practice shapes theory, and the dialogue continues. Both theory and practice remain in a constant state of flux but remain in check by past and current contexts. It isn't change for the sake of change, but change based upon past and present reflections and actions. Change occurs when it is linked to a history and guided by belief rather than haphazardly linked without clear direction. Basically, what we have just described is *dialogue*, an idea for which Bakhtin has much to offer.

Talking With Mikhail Bakhtin: Unpacking Heteroglossia

When typing *heteroglossia*, even we admit that it feels jargonistic, and perhaps it is, although it does provide a shorthand for a complex but critical process. Emerson and Holquist (1981), in the glossary to their translation of *The Dialogic Imagination: Four Essays by M.M. Bakhtin*, describe *heteroglossia* as

> the base condition governing the operation of meaning in any utterance. It is that which insures the primacy of context over text. At any given time, in any given place, there will be a set of conditions—social, historical, meteorological, physiological—that will insure that a word uttered in that place and at that time will have a meaning different than it would not have under any other conditions; all utterances are heteroglot in that they are functions of a matrix of forces practically impossible to recoup, and therefore impossible to resolve. (p. 428)

This description of heteroglossia mirrors Rosenblatt's description of transaction in literature, that meaning is dependent upon any number of factors, and those factors combine through us collectively and individually to generate meaning that is both connected to all other meaning and unique to its context. Or, as Michelle noted, context is everything when it comes to understanding.

Emerson and Holquist (1981) continue their discussion:

> Heteroglossia is as close a conceptualization as is possible of that locus where centripetal and centrifugal forces collide; as such, it is that which a systematic linguistics must always suppress. (p. 428)

This idea of centripetal and centrifugal forces is particularly useful to us as an inquiry community. According to Bakhtin (1981), social forces continually try to stabilize language so that communication can occur for a greater number of people across a wider landscape. However, the concern is that these centripetal forces—forces that pull toward the center and unification—

will reify or petrify the language, harden it into stone, leaving what Bakhtin has likened to the "naked corpse of the word, from which we can learn nothing at all about the social situation or the fate of a given word in life" (p. 292). Without context to provide meaning, language is an empty shell.

Countering these unifying forces are centrifugal forces—forces that pull away from the center toward diversification. Whereas centripetal forces seem fueled by dominant social consensus, centrifugal forces respond to the needs and actions of smaller collectives and individuals. Although they keep languages vibrant and in flux, centrifugal forces run the risk of pulling the language in too many directions, rendering it useless.

As we saw with the concepts of efferent and aesthetic reading as well as thought and action, the ideal situation for language lies not at either extreme, but at heteroglossia, the point where the opposing tensions allow language enough stability that communication is fluid and widespread but provide enough diversification to allow for local input and regeneration. Importantly, all three concepts—transaction, praxis, and heteroglossia—try to reconcile that which is personal with that which is social. Communicating, learning, and inquiring are social acts as much as they are individual acts, and it is difficult, if not impossible, to divine where one ends and the other begins.

Perhaps the easiest way to picture heteroglossia is to imagine a tug of war. On one side of the action, the rope is unified and pulled by a composite of defenders of the mainstream power code. On the other side, the rope has frayed into any number of individual fibers, each pulled by an individual seeking to use the language in new and unique ways. Somewhere above a cosmic mud puddle, a ribbon of language flutters, now pulled more to this side, now pulled more to that. But from a Bakhtinian stance, the object of the game is not to pull either side into the mud, but instead to keep up enough tension to run the game in perpetuity.

Building on the idea of centripetal and centrifugal forces acting upon language, social psychologists Hermans and Kempen (1993) argue that because our individual identities are constructed through language, then those identities are subject to the same forces that unify and diversify language. Individuals simultaneously present a unified identity to the world while entertaining an ongoing dialogue with a range of identities, all of which come to the surface at varying times. Andrea Pintaone-Hernandez (2002), while working on her master's thesis, suggested that communities, being composed of individuals, respond to their own centripetal and centrifugal tensions. As such, communities should seek consensus of purpose yet need to be open to the needs of individuals.

Within this framework, Bakhtin argues that response is not a choice. As users of language engage in language transactions, we respond—always. Even the lack of a response is a response. Simultaneously, meaning is always in flux, irrevocably tied to the context surrounding it. As Bakhtin (1986) noted, there is "no such thing as an isolated utterance" (p. 136); something always has been uttered before and something will follow. Perhaps more important, there "can be neither a first nor a last meaning; it always exists among other meanings as a link in a chain of meaning" (p. 146). Therefore, meaning has a social and historical context, but it also has space for an individual response within present and future contexts. Once again, centripetal and centrifugal forces are at play.

The power and possibility of these ideas held our attention as a learning community, and, true to Bakhtin's ideas, they have been realized in collective and individual ways. Possibly one aspect we all valued, however, is the opportunity for dialogue and response within the large cohort. As we will show more clearly in chapter 6, our ongoing dialogue about critical inquiry and inquiry communities helped us create a focus for our work, but that focus encapsulated a range of ideas, perspectives, and cultural vantages. If we weren't always successful in acting on the diversity of perspective, we were, at least, more successful at getting that diversity into the discussion.

We also felt it was important to inquire in ways that recognized the process we were all taking part in, to see our understandings as connections in an ongoing mesh of connections. If meaning is built upon meaning, then it was important for us to layer our work in ways that helped us to see the links across our work and within the larger field of literacy education. The nested quality of our community and the shared writing of this book, particularly in chapters 3, 4, and 5, are manifestations of our attempts to see meaning as shared and in flux. The idea of talking about understandings in our work, rather than findings, indicated our intent to position our work within the centripetal and centrifugal forces that Bakhtin described, to acknowledge a need for some degree of certainty while also acknowledging the fluidity of that position.

■ What These Theories Meant for Our Inquiries

Before we end this chapter, we feel it important to describe how we did what we did and how these theories informed our choices about teaching, research, and working together. As previously noted, we decided upon a nested framework of small cohorts working within a large cohort and of individual inquiries connecting to other inquiries, with both the individual and group inquiries being visible, yet neither being dominant.

In addition, our methods (see Appendix B) needed to reflect process-oriented work. We wanted to be able to enter into dialogue with data in ways that would allow us to shift our questions, approaches, and understandings as it seemed prudent based upon our varied encounters in our classrooms. In short, we wanted to transact with our data. Consequently, our work was qualitative in nature with individuals and small cohorts using methods of gathering and collecting data that applied to their needs.

As a result, some of us, but perhaps not all of us, conducted interviews, gathered student work, video- and audiotaped our classes, or kept teaching journals. To a degree, we all used some form of observational notes. In keeping with our desire to flatten hierarchies and gain multiple perspectives, many of us shared these notes online, and all of us shared some aspect of our data with our small cohorts and the large cohort. Some of us traveled to one another's classrooms, acting as another set of eyes to record and give different interpretations of what we saw occurring there.

When we met in small cohorts or as a large cohort, we frequently used a variation of oral inquiry processes (Himley, 2000) to identify themes and patterns in what we had collected. These processes allow educators to systemically inquire into data in ways that foster multiple perspectives and description rather than prescription. Our methods of analysis, like our methods of gathering, reflected our desire to transact, think, and act on our work in ways that kept individuals and our large cohort in dialogue. It was through such analysis that the themes of community, responsibility, and risk taking were identified and further explored.

Finally, to protect confidentiality, we have used pseudonyms throughout the book for all students mentioned, as well as teachers, except, of course, when referring to ourselves.

The first two chapters of the book have provided a sketch—but really nothing more—of our inquiry community and the concerns and influences that held us in process. A more detailed and overarching view of our inquiry community and how we worked can be found in chapter 6. However, starting with the next chapter, we'll begin filling in the details of the participants and inquiries of each of the three small cohorts, resulting in, if not a complete picture, certainly a fuller representation of our work and subsequent understandings.

CHAPTER 3

Creating Community
by Embracing Tensions

Stories of Our Questions
The Community Cohort

At the time of this study, Amanda Siegel was a first-year teacher with a fourth- and fifth-grade classroom at Dr. Howard Elementary School, Champaign, Illinois, USA; Elizabeth Hogan was a high school English teacher at Centennial High School, Champaign, with eight years of experience teaching high school English; Ellen Elrick was starting her second year of teaching as a second-grade teacher, also at Dr. Howard Elementary School, Champaign; and Eurydice Bouchereau Bauer was a teacher educator at the University of Illinois, Champaign. The following passages are the stories of their questions.

Elizabeth Hogan. A few years ago I took a graduate class about using inquiry as a classroom methodology. I was interested in how inquiry was used specifically in science classes, yet I was an English teacher and wanted to learn more about how I could use it in English. I loved the idea of organizing classes around big ideas and genuine whole-class questions. When I compared how I used questions in the classroom with how questions function in my real life, it occurred to me that many of my questions about life ranged from very practical (Where is the best place to go to get my car fixed?) to more esoteric (What is a good life?) questions. I wondered about the following questions: What would class be like if students and teachers alike had a genuine place to explore a range of questions? How could I plan for and structure teaching and learning around inquiry? At a National Council of Teachers of English conference, I learned more about the use of Socratic seminars (using open-ended questions in the literature classroom to connect literature to the real world through dilemmas). Also, I read a few articles about Socratic cafes being held in cities on the west coast of the United States and Canada. My question then became the following: How would using Socratic seminars in a cotaught English class affect my students' literacy skills?

Amanda Siegel. Before starting my research on critical inquiry pedagogy, I felt like I was preparing for a great discussion around books when I prepared my small-group reading lessons. However, when I reflected on the kinds of participation that were actually taking place in my fourth- and fifth-grade class among students, I was disappointed. My students were answering my questions, but our discussion was limited to only this type of teacher-to-student interaction. I wanted to learn how to engage my students in a discussion in which they explored their own questions and used their peers as resources. I was interested in giving them more responsibility for the development and direction of the dialogue. I questioned what kind of reading instruction would create this depth of student participation to reach genuine levels of discussion.

As a result, I chose to focus on my small-group reading instruction because I knew my current practices were not promoting students' thinking beyond basic comprehension. I knew my students were capable of producing a better analysis of our readings and could go beyond the text to explore bigger ideas seeded within the stories.

Eurydice Bouchereau Bauer. My first question—What does classroom interaction look like in my undergraduate classroom?—grew out of my interest to better understand the type of discussion necessary to sustain inquiry in general and in undergraduate classrooms in particular. A key component of inquiry, and by extension critical inquiry pedagogy, involves dealing with what Lindfors (1999) calls the "double bind" (p. 15). She purports that through each act of inquiry, we engage in a "wonderfully delicate balance, a perfect tension, between our urge to understand (which leads us to impose) and our urge to maintain relationships (which leads us not to impose)" (p. 15). In the case of preservice teachers in my classes, I believed there was a tension between their need to deeply understand what literacy teaching and learning is about (their own inquiry) and their need to get through the program "with good grades," which had implications for their relationship with one another and with me. All of this speaks to the need for a particular type of community that will allow them the time to explore these tensions. For me, closely examining the nature of our discussion provided me with a window into understanding the extent to which I was assisting or hindering their critical inquiry into literacy and their exploration of the tensions associated with that stance.

My second question—How might teachers investigating their own inquiry at a school level be supported?—relates more closely to my work with Amanda and Ellen at their schools. I had a unique opportunity to interact with them and other teachers in their building, which raised a number of questions for me regarding how to best approach and support teacher inquiry at a school level and the possible implication for students' learning. I wanted to better understand what it would take to create the sort of community we created in our large and small cohorts at a school level.

Ellen Elrick. My question originally was, How do second graders see themselves as writers? I had chosen this question because I wanted to focus on my writing instruction. As a second-year teacher, I felt my writing instruction was my weakest instructional area and I wanted to dramatically improve it. I knew the inquiry project would force me to reflect on my practice and analyze it. In addition, I would have the perspective and expertise of other practitioners to further inform my teaching as well as my second graders' thoughts on their developing identities as writers.

However, as the school year progressed, I found I had abandoned my question. I believe this happened because I struggled to enact writing instruction as I had envisioned it. My intention was to strive toward a writers' workshop approach where students worked independently on individual writing projects each day and I guided their writing in individual conferences and in minilessons on writing. However, that plan was not unfolding as I had hoped, so rather than dwell on my inadequacies, I glossed over the subject of writing instruction. In lieu of that struggle, I centered on my reading instruction, in which I was experiencing more success. Thus, what evolved from my project of critical inquiry pedagogy was a narrative of my reading instruction and its impact on classroom interactions around texts.

On the first day of school, students are entering a room where there is no community yet. Everybody is going to have a chance to inform what kind of community it's going to be. The teacher has some rules for rule making, and the school has some norms about what a classroom should or should not look like, but everyone is starting on the same day. Everyone puts a foot in the door. It's exciting, the idea of developing the trust and comfort level in the room to be able to inquire, to get students to a comfort level to ask questions, and to learn from each other without feeling intimidated or ignorant or that they are going to be put down for what they do not know is exciting. (Ellen Elrick)

Ellen captures the essence of a new class forming at the beginning of the school year, with all the potential and inherent complexities that exist when different voices must come to learn together as a community. Likewise, creating our critical inquiry literacy group for teachers gave each of us a chance to learn what kind of community we—the members of this small cohort—wanted to create. Given our diverse backgrounds and points of reference—Eurydice Bouchereau Bauer, teacher educator; Amanda Siegel, a fourth- and fifth-grade teacher; Ellen, a second-grade teacher; and Elizabeth Hogan, a veteran high school English teacher—we recognized the need for focusing attention on establishing and defining community in nontraditional ways.

Our definition of *community* extended beyond the traditional view, in which the group emphasizes commonality and ignores points of tension. We knew from the beginning that such a naive definition of community would be insufficient for describing our work together on critical inquiry pedagogy and our efforts to bring this to our students. Instead, our community capitalized on the tensions that were inherent in our varied roles, thoughts, and dispositions. That is not to say that a teacher could not engage in critical inquiry pedagogy on her own; nor is it to say that a community could not develop around another shared interest. However, for our small cohort, the dynamism was fertile ground for working against the status quo of traditional teacher-fronted classrooms and for fully reflecting on our goals for teaching and learning. Within our range of teaching experience—novice teachers, a veteran teacher, and a university professor—we worked for a common goal: to transform our teaching practices through critical inquiry pedagogy and authentic human interaction. Our genuine need to know and desire to share fueled this exploration. Our goal in this chapter is to tell how we created a cohort that is authentic and is based on genuine needs, while seeking to enact critical inquiry among ourselves and in the classrooms where we taught.

Most of our time together during the first year of the study was spent establishing "shared meaning" through our conversations; after reading texts on critical inquiry and teacher research, we would offer our intentions for our respective classrooms. We wanted to create a space where we could really discuss the issues surrounding literacy and interrupt the cautious discourse often found in learning communities. For this to occur, we needed to accomplish three things:

1. establish a strong community of learners that would allow for vigorous exploration of our collective background of thought, our personal dispositions, the nature of our shared intention, and the rigid features of our individual and collective assumptions (Isaacs, 1993);

2. conduct self-studies to better understand the ways in which we supported or hindered our students' exploration of their understanding of themselves as learners; and

3. encourage our students to examine how they construct their understanding of what constitutes literate behavior.

In sharing our process for establishing community and our learning, we are not suggesting that we have arrived at a final understanding of critical inquiry or how it translates into pedagogy. Instead, we view ourselves as on a journey with our burgeoning understanding of inquiry as our guide. In the remainder of the chapter, we present how we addressed our small-cohort tensions, our framework for understanding our community, and our individual efforts toward establishing community and critical inquiry pedagogy. We use our stories to show how, throughout our investigation, we were in search of authentic teaching and learning.

■ Small-Cohort Tensions

As the four of us began to establish roles within our cohort, a tension emerged between the push to equalize our responsibility and the natural tendency to rely on a guide with recognized knowledge. We knew that all of us had something to bring to the small cohort, but Eurydice was the only small-cohort member with extensive experience in data collection and teacher research. For Ellen and Amanda, this was their first foray as classroom action researchers. Elizabeth completed National Board Certification the prior year, and that process required intense personal reflection on her instruction, but it was an individual investigation, whereas now she was part of a research community. Eurydice's research on classroom instruction and assessment during the last eight years was a potential resource for us, but this automatically put her in a more knowledgeable position, a position she at times resisted and at other times had to embrace.

We took turns hosting our monthly three-hour meetings in our homes. At an October 2002 meeting hosted by Elizabeth, Eurydice became aware that her expertise might influence the power structure of the community, and she initiated shared responsibility from the beginning.

Eurydice: May I make a little suggestion? Whoever is hosting our month-ly meeting should also lead the discussions during that session. This way, I am not always the one doing it. I don't want you guys saying, "Oh, she will take care of it."

Amanda: What else is the person responsible for? [pause] Maybe they should give us notes.

Elizabeth: That's me. Whoever is hosting it, right?

Amanda: So that person reports back to the whole group [large cohort].

Eurydice: We need to figure out what to do with the book [we are read-ing]. How will we use it? We want to feel like this will be our most productive year. So, how can we make use of each other and help each other?

Elizabeth: How about I jump in and say we talk a little about the book and observations so that we can take care of that at the beginning.... [Elizabeth continues to talk about how she read the index, flipped through the book, and found some practical advice about collecting data.] Maybe we should agree on what sections to read. [The cohort agrees on a reading assignment.]

Eurydice: Maybe we should talk about our data [collected from our stu-dents] today. We need to know each other's data so that we can help each other...I don't know; it's just a thought.

Elizabeth: So let's go around the room and share. [Elizabeth shares hers first.] Ellen, what have you collected? [Ellen, Amanda, and Eurydice share what they have collected.]

After everyone reported on her data and plans for further investigation, our attempt at maintaining equality began to break down. Even though Eurydice extended an invitation for sharing responsibility with regard to learning, her research background eventually began to influence the meeting.

Eurydice: Can I jump in, if you don't mind, and make a little suggestion? As I listen to what has been shared, I am a little concerned that

there might be a discrepancy between what [data you are col-
lecting] and what you're saying you want to learn. I guess I feel
the need to put that out there. I want to make sure that at the
end of the year all of us have something meaningful to look at.
So, I need to hear again what it is you are doing [collecting]
and what you want to learn so I can better match what I hear
you are doing to what it is you are getting at.

After listening to the discussion Eurydice realized that Elizabeth and Ellen
seemed unsure about which aspect of their classrooms should become their
data. When talking to Elizabeth later in the meeting, Eurydice remarked:

Eurydice: You could look at [how your students' skills change] over the
            year. But, if you are looking at changes, you need to find a sys-
            tematic way of getting that information. So, besides videotap-
            ing, maybe your reflections could be part of what you focus
            on....You might also want to focus your reflection in your jour-
            nal to keep track of things. I am wondering why you chose the
            four students you selected.

Ellen: My whole class is totally interesting!

Eurydice: Yes, but you cannot collect data from the whole class. You will
            have too much data, and you might not get the information
            that you want. It might also get overwhelming. We could help
            you get started with one area, maybe reading, and you could re-
            port to us as you look at your findings.... I think we need a set
            format so that we have an agenda when we report back to each
            other. If we have a three-hour meeting, we could have one hour
            on reporting and suggestions, a second hour looking at the text,
            and a third hour looking at data.

As the discussion returned to Ellen's data and goals, Eurydice realized that
Ellen was collecting many samples from her students but was not sure what
to do with the data. Also, it occurred to Eurydice that Ellen might need to be
more precise about what she wanted to study. Eurydice attempted to direct
the discussion to Ellen's data collection.

Eurydice: Maybe we can brainstorm...I don't need to provide the words
            of wisdom here.

Elizabeth: Ellen, what do you do during writing conferences now with your
            students? [Ellen explained, and the conversation continued.]

Amanda: [Directed at Eurydice] So, what do you want me to have for
            next time?

Eurydice:	Wait, it's not what I want. Notice the way she phrased that remark. I am feeling like you are one of my students asking, "What do you want me to do?"
Elizabeth:	[Directed at Amanda] It might be interesting to see the charts you created with your class.
Amanda:	OK, Eurydice, research? [Eurydice then presented her data.]

This conversation demonstrated how we (Elizabeth, Ellen, and Amanda) wanted to learn from Eurydice's research background, and as much as she wanted us to share the authority, her knowledge was necessary to lead us to the type of data we wanted to collect. Eurydice struggled with letting us find out on our own how to continue the research because she recognized the need to focus our inquiries to achieve effective data collection. At this point, we accepted her expertise in this area and let Eurydice lead us through the research experience.

If we were all novice researchers, we would not have had the same conversation about what research methods would yield our specific goals. We could have been satisfied with our data collection but worried less about what the data has to say to the data collector and others later on, risking the possibility that our understandings would be limited to our individual anecdotes.

As we reflected on this dialogue, we realized that Eurydice's role as expert researcher leading the way was more pronounced at the beginning of the year when she was worried that we were considering everything that we collected was data and felt the need to bring more structure to our endeavor. We found it interesting that, once we moved beyond setting up the data collection, her role as leader was less pronounced. Perhaps the primary reason for this shift was that we all had specific data to bring to our cohort sessions and, therefore, needed her guidance less for that. The real shift in our work dynamics came when we had to write for our presentation at the National Council of Teachers of English conference and, later, for this book. Although Eurydice was willing to draw from our individual writings to write the presentation, we decided that the pinnacle of our success would be marked by our ability to work on more equal footing with her. After all, we had done a fair amount of writing in the past and felt comfortable with our writing ability in general; however, we all were not sure of our ability to write about our research. Our writing endeavors brought us closer to where we wanted to be in regard to leveling the usual hierarchies among university, high school, and elementary school teachers.

As Dewey (1916) and Bakhtin (1981) contend, there is always a tension between the needs of the individual and the community, which results in constant negotiation and adjustments. This negotiation is inherently tied to the individual's social interaction as part of the community. As we engaged in sustained dialogues within our small cohort, we formed the basis for our continued classroom research agenda. Engaging in a community that we designed around "shared meaning" allowed us to examine and reexamine what we wanted to create for students in our individual classrooms, while recognizing that just like us, our students brought different kinds of expertise to the classroom.

Teachers have a desire to create an environment where both teacher and students can build on what they are learning about one another. This ongoing teacher need for balance was ever present in our monthly cohort meetings and in our classrooms. Similar to the tensions we experienced in establishing a working community in our small cohort, the tension between our function as teachers who are responsible for our students' intellectual development and academic achievement and who are committed to the motivating power of students' inquiry affected our teaching roles in the classroom.

■ Bakhtin's Heteroglossia: A Framework for Our Understanding of Community

Our approach to understanding the creation and sustenance of our small cohort and teaching and doing critical inquiry pedagogy builds on Bakhtin's literary theories (1981) and applies to his notion of heteroglossia—that is, "the various influencing contexts that influence text" (p. 428). Bakhtin argues that all verbal interaction is social and that all language will have different meanings dependent on their context. This is why a reader can have a different interpretation of the same novel upon his or her second reading of it. Language and meaning, therefore, are in flux. This notion of heteroglossia proved meaningful for developing community both among the four of us and within our specific classrooms.

As noted in chapter 2, one finds within heteroglossia centripetal forces—that is, culturally unifying and centralizing discourse vital to creating a common language—and centrifugal forces—that is, decentralizing and dispersing forces in any language and culture (Bakhtin, 1981). As a result of the heteroglossia of our inquiry cohort in which centripetal (i.e., common texts, personal connections, and mutual trust and respect) and centrifugal (i.e., varied voices, backgrounds, and agendas) forces were allowed to transact, we as teachers were able to grow a certain "tolerance for uncertainty" (Clark, 2001, p. 179) within our small cohort and then within our specific classrooms. In essence, a nesting effect developed in which we tried out our thinking and ideas about critical inquiry pedagogy among the four of us, and then sought to bring them to the classroom, only to recast notions of critical inquiry pedagogy when we once again met with one another. This constant revisiting of our ideas led us to understand Bakhtin's notion that language is never static and is always context-bound, and as Eurydice noted, "it is our multiple voices [both centralizing and dispersing] that came together to create something new in our inquiry cohort and our classrooms. That something new is community."

Hierarchical power relationships usually define relationships within the classroom as well as relationships within a K–12/university relationship. Traditional professors and teachers usually impart knowledge in the form of one-way communication. All of us are affected by the cultural notion of a professor's and public school teacher's discourse. Our study was affected by the fact that Eurydice had more experience with research and could mentor us (Amanda, Elizabeth, and Ellen) to become better beginning researchers. After a while, we took on more responsibility. Likewise, we entered our classrooms with more knowledge than our students on school curriculum objectives. This knowledge and experience can help us to empower our students as long as we do not overrely on our authority and squelch students' curiosity with authoritarian teaching. Instead, we have to mentor our students so they can take control of their own learning.

Bakhtin says this transmitted spoken language in a traditional teacher–student relationship cannot be represented in a heteroglossia; it is, as he describes it, "authoritative discourse" defined by "its inertia, its semantic finiteness and calcification, the degree to which it is hard-edged, a thing in its own right, the impermissibility of any free stylistic development in relation to it" (Bakhtin, 1981, p. 344). Unlike centripetal forces, it does not serve to unify the culture, but it is used to preserve knowledge in a static form rather than to acknowledge the dynamic interaction of language inherent in a heteroglossia. In contrast to this "authoritative discourse," we found an ability to pursue within our inquiry cohort an "internally persuasive discourse" (Bakhtin, 1981, p. 346) that is defined by our willingness to examine the context that gave rise to that discourse and how it was dialogized, which allowed us the opportunity to continually examine newer ways to make meaning.

In the next section, we present our classroom efforts at supporting critical inquiry pedagogy. Much of what we have learned can be captured by the theme "examining the social context of teaching leads to the reconfiguration of community norms." Throughout this section, we highlight the tensions that were inherent in our interactions with one another and with our students.

■ Portraits of the Social Context of Teaching Lead to the Reconfiguration of Community Norms

One of the issues of creating community in the classroom is the way in which teachers traditionally position themselves with respect to students. Teachers stereotypically are authoritarians dictating various aspects of the classroom culture from the nature of interactions to the structure of the space (Mehan, 1978). Teachers in this role enact an authoritative discourse; there is no dialogue between teacher and student about classroom culture, but, rather, teachers dictate it. Before we began to explore our roles as teachers wanting to enact critical inquiry pedagogy, it was our tendency to enter our classroom interactions with students using an authoritative discourse. Through a controlling stance, we attempted to circumvent tensions while not realizing we needed students' individual stances and the tensions created by their stances to have critical discourse.

Although we attempted to create inquiry lessons, we weren't able to completely escape aspects of the authoritarian role. For example, Elizabeth initially viewed her role as a classroom teacher as the provider of important ideas that would ignite students' interest in critically examining their future. Amanda identified key elements of classroom discourse and then sought to control them in an effort to better engage students in their learning. Eurydice approached and framed her teaching within a sociocultural viewpoint but wanted to do more to recognize and include students' needs and their working understanding of the issues to reshape her instruction. Ellen framed her discussions around teacher-centered reading skills that she felt were vital to reading comprehension in an attempt to improve students' understanding of texts. Throughout the remainder of the chapter we draw upon our individual cases to tell what we learned about community with regard to teaching our students.

Elizabeth's Classroom: Asking the Big Questions

My original research question was, What is the effect of organizing a co-taught senior literature and rhetoric class around big inquiry questions? This includes the questions, What does it mean to be a human being? and What will it mean to be an adult? My purpose in organizing my classes around big ideas is to engage students, who are on the cusp of adulthood, in discussions around literature and writing that connected to their lives. I want this class to provide them with something significant, something they can use to improve their reading, writing, thinking, and speaking for academic purposes and beyond, but also for something more soulful, such as How will I function as an adult in this complicated world? The young woman I was as a senior in high school was like a doppelganger this entire year, shadowing me, whispering to me: They need more than anyone can provide; they need strength and resilience; this student doesn't have anyone watching out for him or her; this student is living alone; this student is working 60 hours a week; this student is living out of her car. The truth is that although I was in honors classes when I was their age, I was terrified, too. Now as a teacher, I wonder if addressing these big questions might engage students in an inquiry that would give them the tools to manage and engage fully in their futures.

The first-semester literature class that I taught seemed perfect for examining the question, What does it mean to be a human being? We strengthened our skills for reading *Hamlet* (Shakespeare, 2004) by reading stories such as *Like Water for Chocolate* (Esquivel, 1992), and *Oedipus the King* (Sophocles, 2004). I taught the heuristic portion of the Socratic seminar by modeling it first with the stories. I was reminded of what Bob Fecho said in a meeting of the large cohort about inquiry not being something he does "just on Fridays." But for me, I did start with doing the seminars just on Fridays. I never fully transformed the classroom into an inquiry-based classroom, but I did integrate inquiry into the classroom through the use of Friday Socratic seminars. At the outset of the Socratic seminar, I was responsible for creating the questions. I posed open-ended questions that I thought would be interesting to the students personally and that would lead to more questions, but I was aware that initially I was very much in control of the agenda, which reflected a tension I feel about teacher authority. I've since wondered what would have happened if, from the onset of the Socratic seminars, I had asked the students to pose the essential questions themselves? I feared that the students in my class would not have asked the kind of questions that would sustain class discussion; therefore, we would have been left without a substantial lesson plan.

The classroom I taught that year was fairly diverse in terms of race and gender. In addition, several students needed individual educational plans to support their learning disabilities, Also, like most classrooms, the willingness of students to read and discuss literature varied to some degree. Noting that the students had read "Do Not Go Gently Into That Good Night" by Thomas (1952/2004), "An Occurrence at Owl Creek Bridge" by Bierce (1891/2004), and "The Lottery" by Jackson (1948/2004), I provided the following seminar questions: What is a healthy view of life and death? Are we more responsible to ourselves or to our community? I asked the students to connect back to the text, in addition to making text-to-self connections. Text-to self connections allow the students to connect their lives to the text, while connecting to the text keeps them grounded in the reading and forces students to use textual evidence when talking about the book.

Although these questions provoked interesting student responses, the heuristic portion of the Socratic seminar provided the space for student-generated questions. One student, Jay, said, "I know this is deep, but what if this is it? What if when you die, you die?" In my role as a teacher, I said to my students, "This is also a topic to discuss with your parents and which can relate to religious beliefs, but if what you say is true, you will not be conscious of being dead, so there is no need to fear." I felt that I needed to say that rather than throwing the question back to the class. Part of inquiry is going out on a limb, and no one will take you there faster than a teenager. I was grateful that he was willing to nudge us into risky territory, but I wanted to provide a comforting, parental response. In retrospect, I was trying to shield them from midday existential angst. Perhaps I should have let them explore this question more in depth.

The students' responses to the question of whether one is more responsible to oneself or to others was interesting. Blake, a student in the class, mentioned that our duty to community depended on whether or not the community was supportive of us. One student brought up the fact that Mrs. Hutchison in "The Lottery" went against her community only when it was too late, and, basically, for selfish reasons. All of us questioned why the protagonist of "An Occurrence at Owl Creek Bridge," Peyton Farhquhar, would have blown up the bridge if he knew he was at risk for execution. His duty to his community was greater than the urge to preserve his own life. Louis, another student in the class, said, "If you don't take care of yourself, how are you going to take care of your community?" Jay's reaction was classic: "You don't say anything all during class, then you come up with that?" Although the students based their conversations in the class on teacher-created questions, students responded openly and found a space for asking their own questions. I suspected that this openness might have occurred because the questions I posed were questions I did not have answers for. Therefore, I, too, could participate in the exploration for understanding.

Amanda's Classroom: Engendering Authentic Discussion

Sometimes teaching can be just like a performance with the teacher as the director. Being a novice teacher, I was somewhat naive and thought in terms of staging a successful inquiry lesson. To me, it seemed like designing a theater in the round: I picked a good story for my upper-grades elementary students to read, selected a cast, and used a circular table to set the scene. I thought the dialogue then should occur and become a thought-provoking, in-depth script. However, I soon realized that sometimes a grand plan can still be a box-office flop.

For example, I chose a magazine article that was rich with information on the merit of cloning. I wrote lots of open-ended questions and picked a diverse group for a small-group discussion. There *was* going to be a great discussion on the merit of cloning because I was prepared for one. The magazine was full of great information students should be wondering about, right? To begin, we focused on an article about genetically cloning animals. After reading, a number of students were asking lots of questions, and I thought, "Alright. Now we are inquiring!" Then I realized that the students directed all the questions to me, and most of them were different types of comprehension questions: How do they put the egg in the cat? What is genetics? You mean they put chemicals in the cat? However, my agenda was to engage them in a discussion on whether cloning animals was a good idea, not to explain how it is done.

On the other hand, this was an appropriate time for me to remember what Lindfors (1999) said about inquiry, "You can't ask questions about something you know nothing about. The only question I can ask about nuclear science is 'what is it?'" (p. 93). This is what happened to my students. Cloning was so foreign to them, they needed to first understand what it was before they could wonder about its worth. Well, wasn't this my opportunity as a teacher to get my point across? So I stepped onto my soapbox and shared the scientific and personal theories about the benefits and dangers of cloning organs, creating replacement pets, and needing genetic diversity. When I stepped down, the students didn't have anything to say. Did I say too much? This was not what I had envisioned; I acted as a one-woman show instead of the director of my students' inquiries. Why did I define my role as an omniscient provider of knowledge? What would have happened if I hadn't supplied all the answers? How can I prepare my students to engage in more interactive discussions?

At the onset of my investigation, I planned my lessons around teacher-generated, open-ended questions that I felt were important, such as Was it a good idea to clone the cat? and Why would people want to clone their pets? Framing questions in this way did not elicit the responses I expected. I heard, "[The article] says the families wanted another cat," or "[The article] says it's safe." "Authentic" conversation did not occur. This sounded more like a comprehension check than the exchange of thoughts and wonderments I had planned for initially.

In contrast, when students were given a real opportunity to explore literature without teacher-directed questions, the students found the space to venture into genuine inquiry. Once when I was short on time to prepare, I had not created a list of preplanned questions to complement the lesson. To my surprise, the students demonstrated their knowledge and capability to guide the conversation by contributing their own questions. Adding to their depth of discussion were better choices in texts that I chose that were more appropriate to their interests and experiences. Articles about familiar but bizarre occurrences in nature lent themselves to real opportunities for students to seek understanding. The following discussion occurred when introducing an article about the mystery of Big Foot (a mythological beast) to my third graders:

Amanda: Turn to page 62, read the title, and look at the picture.

Amy: Big Foot? Is he real?

Katie: I think he's famous.

David: Oh yeah, they named a gas station after him. He was in a movie once with Donald Duck.

Brian: He was in the Simpsons, too! He turned out to be a nice monster.

Amy: I think Big Foot is the king or queen of the apes or gorillas.

Gary: People say we used to be apes. Apes talk, too.... I have seen them on [television] doing sign language, dancing...and holding a baby gorilla.

Katie: I think Big Foot is real. Why would people make up stories?

Brian: So they can scare you.

Gary: I think Big Foot is dead now because if he lived 1,000 years ago, he would be a living fossil.

Amy: What if those were children of Big Foot in the movies...you know, like Big Foot Juniors?

When the lesson was over, I recognized the difference in the student responses when my voice posed the questions and when the students shaped the discussion. They showed true interest and were anxious to converse with one another and to read the text to find out more. This dialogue demonstrated their search for their own and collective understanding of Big Foot rather than the teacher directly explaining speculations and checking for comprehension. The "I think..." statements revealed individual theories that encouraged the group to connect ideas and push their thinking farther to examine and hypothesize about Big Foot's existence. These students created a space to share and wonder that set the stage for a more personal and genuine discourse around the text. In addition, their authentic comments and questions indicated to me their familiarity with Big Foot and from where they were pulling their knowledge. Awareness of their prior knowledge and group understanding also gave me the opportunity to build greater relevance between the text readings, their experiences, and their inquiries.

After recognizing the success of a lesson I did not control, I am left wondering: Would the students have been so interested in exploring their understanding if I posed the original question? Or would they have been more concerned about answering the teacher correctly? These types of interactions with my students guided my investigation of how I might create a balance between the students' questioning of text and how my questioning could better support their efforts. After all, when the students were given the space to question Big Foot's existence, they owned the discussion, and I wanted them to have ownership for their learning. This notion of whether discussions can take place when the teacher directs questions is also an idea that Elizabeth explored during her Socratic seminars.

Eurydice's Classroom: Examining Issues of Diversity

I constructed my undergraduate courses so that issues of diversity were placed at the center of my instruction, rather than at the periphery or even as an afterthought. For example, the students and I discussed the roles that gender, class, and ethnicity play in students' literacy development in the classroom. As part of two courses on teaching literacy in elementary schools, my students were asked to read texts (i.e., *Dreamkeepers* by Ladson-Billings, 1994, and *Reading and Writing in More Than One Language* by Franklin, 1999) representing various viewpoints as well as engaging in written and oral discussions regarding the intersection between teaching literacy and cultural diversity among schoolchildren. Although I wanted to establish community through texts, I never once asked my students for their input on how to explore these topics or about what texts we would read.

I viewed my role as a teacher educator as one who led my students to think and understand how they construct their knowledge of the world (Vygotsky, 1934/1978, 1934/1986). For example, I provided them with opportunities to develop certain skills that would lead them to teach their future students using a constructivist framework. That is, students have an opportunity to explore how they construct and what they construct in the name of literacy. We accomplished this through the different reflective activities they engaged in (e.g., a reflective log). I worked with my students to develop their practice and content knowledge in literacy, their understanding of what it means to teach diverse learners, and their professional outlook of the teaching field. In my conception of teaching, I emphasized the social context in which learning and literacy emerge, but within this conception, most of the responsibility for orchestrating how learning should take place in the classroom lies with the teacher. Through my interactions with Elizabeth, Amanda, and Ellen, I questioned my teaching by asking what would happen if students had more voice in the classroom? What would our classroom discourse be?

Some of my teacher questions attempted to guide my students' learning by helping them analyze and reflect on their readings. Questions such as How can one become culturally competent in a culture that is not one's own? or Using the readings assigned the last three weeks, how might you present your emerging definition of comprehension? shaped our focus. Some of these questions were meant to help students learn the material better, but I was not convinced that they necessarily pushed them to inquire about the content as a whole and their own personal issues regarding the teaching of literacy. What I found was that these types of open-ended, teacher-generated questions served as a good tool to assess how well students were grappling with the content of literacy but did so on a superficial level.

Other questions that I posed to my students were along the lines of Elizabeth's essential questions; however, the context was different. For example, I asked the students throughout the year to maintain a reflective log on their readings. Not wanting to have the logs be an end in themselves, I asked the students to evaluate their log entries, in a sense asking them to evaluate themselves, midsemester and at the end of the year. I asked the students to evaluate their entries based on content and ability to convey their thoughts to the reader. As the class discussed with me possible issues they examined as part of their evaluation of themselves, they raised questions. These questions were very broad in nature, and the answers, unlike questions I posed to them, were unknown to me. I shared with the students the type of questions previous students posed when doing this type of activity to provide some direction. I made it clear that students would create their own burning questions based on their journal entries. Here are some of the questions that I shared from prior students: How is my current understanding of literacy tied to my previous experiences? Based on the previous entries, where are the holes in my thinking regarding literacy? What is it about my approach to this content that contributes to my struggles with the intersection between literacy and diversity? Essentially, students were using their logs as data. Based on their reading and rereading of their entries, they tried to go beyond the words they wrote to critically examine where they were at the point of the evaluation and where they needed to go. This way, it wasn't just the teacher's job to evaluate and set goals but the students' as well. Students used the raw data and the questions that the raw data generated to write an evaluation of themselves.

Unlike the questions that were meant to simply help students navigate their assigned readings, the questions that stemmed from the students' journals were more provocative and gave better insight into where they were in their knowledge development. Having them share in small groups what they learned from looking at their thoughts on paper also allowed a number of students to find greater meaning in this activity. The goals the students set at the end of this type of writing also provided students with a stronger sense of purpose about what they were going to be learning in the subsequent weeks following the evaluation. I suspected that the students explored their thoughts more deeply when they generated the journal questions because they had more control over the entire process.

Ellen's Classroom: Wondering Engagement With Texts

Given my district's increasing focus on student performance on standardized tests and given my status as a novice teacher, I focused on what I perceived to be essential student literacy skills. I modeled the ways readers interact with text to create meaning and then had students apply these skills in book discussions. For instance, during read-alouds I structured discussions around making text-to-self and text-to-text connections (Miller, 2002). Also, I encouraged students to ask questions, predict, infer, and reflect to improve their overall understanding of text.

While students were engaged with the texts beyond decoding the words, the lens I used to focus our discussions did not capture all my students' wonderings. For example, when I read aloud *Chato's Kitchen* (Soto, 1995), I chose to use the text to explore making predictions. The text lent itself to making predictions, but Soto also wrote it in a distinct voice, a tough, streetwise Latino voice. The voice of the text was very different than my own white, middle class, midwestern U.S. voice. As I was reading, some students giggled when Chato spoke and one student exclaimed, "Ms. Elrick, I didn't know you could talk like that!"

This remark was a perfect invitation to discuss the use of different registers in reading and writing, but I had planned to teach prediction. While I didn't ignore my student's remark, I quickly explained how I was reading it like the author wrote it and that this is how the characters would speak because of their background; they certainly wouldn't speak like me. When I reflected on this incident, I wondered, what would have happened if I had strayed from my agenda to teach prediction as an essential comprehension skill and explored my student's reaction to the author's presentation of a character's language? Missing this opportunity to explore a student's curiosity about a text awoke my interest in using critical inquiry pedagogy to teach literacy.

I felt my reading instruction was improving. Students were not only concerned with getting the words right when reading, but they also were focused on understanding the story. The evidence of the students' thinking about stories was visible on the various charts and other student work hanging on the walls of the classroom. For example, there was a chart comparing and contrasting various trickster tales students had read and a bulletin board filled with drawings that depicted students' mental images from various poems. There was also a chart listing the questions students had as they read *How Many Days to America? A Thanksgiving Story* (Bunting, 1988). The questions ranged from What did the kids do on the boat? to Why did they leave their country? Underneath each question were students' responses. It appeared good learning was happening and my students were engaged with texts beyond simply retelling the story. However, Lindfors (1999) characterizes inquiry interactions as "rough draft talk," (p. 169), and the types of interactions in my room were much like the charts adorning the walls, tidy and structured with everything fitting neatly on the page.

After observing a reading lesson, Eurydice pointed out that my approach to reading instruction—focusing students on only one aspect of the reading—might send the wrong message to students. That is, they should only think about reading in a way that the teacher deems appropriate. Eurydice suggested I allow the students to do more wondering about text.

At first, I balked at this idea. I felt the structure of my reading instruction was necessary because otherwise read-alouds and book discussions degenerated into storytelling hour. For example, when I read aloud *Amazing Grace* (Hoffman, 1991), student talk moved away from the text to whether or not they had watched the same movie on television last night. I couldn't see where the learning was in that type of discourse. Yet on some level, I understood that Eurydice was not asking me to replicate the discussion around *Amazing Grace*. The crux of my dilemma was my need to feel in control, especially as a novice teacher. This type of tension reinforced for me the Bakhtinian (Bakhtin, 1981) tug and pull that often existed between the needs of my students and my needs as a classroom teacher.

With some reservations about how I would handle discussion, I read aloud *A Picture Book of Martin Luther King, Jr.* (Adler, 1989) and, as I read the text, I would occasionally stop and ask the students what they were thinking rather than using carefully thought-out prompts that would promote specific responses to the text. The excerpt from my journal highlights what happened:

> I allowed more of the wondering engagement that was happening with the Martin Luther King [MLK], Jr., books. On Friday when we read *A Picture Book of Martin Luther King, Jr.*, the talk turned to stories about how African Americans were treated "back in the day," but also there was another idea that came up, which was what did [MLK] do to get along with people who openly hated him and tried to kill him.

At first, I viewed stories such as the "back in the day" stories as digressions. However, central to this classroom interaction was the fact that students, in addition to relating events in the text to real-life situations, also were considering the larger social question of race relations discussed in the text. At first, it seemed that the students' talk was getting off task with stories of wrongful treatment of African Americans, but it actually helped lead us to higher level thinking about text and critical issues as evidenced by the students' wondering about how to get along with people who openly hate you. This caused me to rethink what counts as a good lesson.

■ Building on Experiences

The preceding classroom portraits demonstrate how each of us in our small cohort initially structured discourse within our classrooms from an authoritative discourse. What is interesting to note is that our initial efforts were attempts at structuring classrooms for critical inquiry pedagogy, but our monthly discussions of our classroom data revealed the tenacious effect of authoritative discourse operating in our classrooms. The cohort's continued dialogue on critical inquiry pedagogy clarified our understanding of what Bakhtin (1981) meant when he argued that authoritative discourse limits the spaces where students' voices can enter and shape classroom discussions.

As our cohort explored and discussed critical inquiry pedagogy as part of our classroom practice, we became conscious of the guiding power of authentic questions, and we began to wonder whether our students had enough opportunities to ask their own authentic questions. We started to draw parallels between what we were doing in our small cohort and what we needed to do in our classrooms. Specifically, we needed to examine why there was such discrepancy between the type of questions we were asking in our cohort—questions that felt more open-ended, thought provoking, and open to multiple perspectives—and the type of questions we were asking our students and that they were asking of us and one another—questions that often seemed, in both cases, more close-ended, information oriented, and finite in perspective. Across our individual classrooms, we began to explore the role of questions and how they might encourage the building of community.

Just as how we defined ourselves as teachers in the classroom affected the development of our classroom communities, we realized that the types of questions we asked and the space we created for student questioning in the classroom also were vital components for developing a community poised for inquiry. Lindfors (1999) describes the ideal space for inquiry to take place, which seemed to us to be the likely source for students' genuine questions:

> I believe that there is no single human activity more fundamental and powerful in one's learning than inquiry. We hear much about the Zone of Proximal development these days, that particularly promising cognitive area where a child can go further with another's help. This is where inquiry lives. Vygotsky points out that it is neither what the child can do independently already, nor what is way beyond the child's current ability, that is most promising for the child's learning at any given moment. Rather, the place of promise is that area just beyond the child's reach. Acts of inquiry occur at this very place. The child controls the zone through his or her acts of inquiry. These acts bring the helping other—often the teacher—to that perfect place, the going-beyond-with-help place. (p. 20)

Realizing how important students' questions are (see Commeyras & Sumner, 1998, for more discussion) to understanding their grasp on the content and direction of their wondering, while also empowering their participation, led us to look at how to balance teacher-driven and student-driven questions.

■ Steps Toward Authentic Interactions

Amanda, Eurydice, and Elizabeth all gave more control to students with their use of questions. Amanda gave students the opportunity to generate their own questions and guide their own discussion around their queries. Eurydice used both teacher- and student-generated questions in her classroom. She felt that students explored their thoughts more deeply when they posed the questions. Elizabeth posed authentic questions in her Socratic seminar that caused students to raise their own questions in an attempt to answer the larger teacher question—What does it mean to be a human? Ellen moved away from teacher-prescribed interactions with texts to wondering engagement with texts. In each case, the use of student questions introduced what Bakhtin (1981) describes as "internally persuasive discourse" (p. 346) into the classroom. Through questions, students were able to recast the discourse, and they made the discussion more contemporary or relevant to their own need to understand. The interaction became more of a heteroglossia with multiple questions guiding the discussion.

Our concerns over the type of teachers' and students' questions and our teacher roles invariably explored what a "good lesson" should be. We especially struggled to define this within our view of community. Our working definition of community included the acceptance of the tensions associated with the cohort's and individuals' needs. This means that a teacher needs to consider a good lesson within a concern or awareness of community, which invariably means a heteroglossia (various contexts and needs) exists. A *good lesson* from our perspective should involve teachers taking into account their students and possible interactions with one another and their teachers, as well as their own goals when thinking about the direction for their lessons. Therefore, educators should not embrace generic lessons and instead should frame their teaching goals around the uniqueness of the class.

■ In Search of Authenticity

Throughout our investigation, we wanted to understand and clarify how community—comprising the teacher's role, types of questioning, and our working view of a good lesson—might be linked to our need for honest interaction within our small cohort and our own classrooms. We defined *authentic interaction* as interactions that are driven by the need to know and share. More often than not, teachers' interactions with students fit traditional patterns of teacher questioning and students answering (Cazden, 1988), yet authentic interaction for critical inquiry pedagogy seems to depend on teachers and students communicating in ways that disrupt these traditional patterns. What conditions, then, need to be present for authentic interactions?

Across our small cohort and within our own classrooms, we realized that procedures, heuristics, and structures, at least initially, needed to be present for authentic interaction to occur. For example, Elizabeth taught her students to use the Socratic seminar, Ellen used graphic organizers, and Eurydice used students' reflective logs as entries into their own investigations of themselves as learners. We used these initial scaffolds to develop common ground among diverse groups of inquirers. As our classes developed into communities, the structures became less visible but just as supportive. For example, within the structure of the Socratic seminar, authentic interaction flourished during a seminar on *Like Water for Chocolate* (Esquivel, 1992) when Jay provided a response to the essential question, "How can one overcome social inequalities or a difficult family life?" by beginning an extended explanation of how "fun" and "laughing" can help you overcome adversity:

James: The whole family gets together one day of the year. That's always Thanksgiving, and the thing that always comes up, I don't like this, we always talk about, like, tragedies in our family.... That hurts me 'cause, like, my dad and then my grandpa really were the...two important people in my [life], and my brother, he left me, but then [while]...we're still talking about them, it just becomes a joke, like, do you remember back when, when my dad did such and such, and you know? We get to talking about the fun times. And really, you don't even think about the fact that they are gone....

Elizabeth: Yeah.

Jay: 'Cause you can reminisce about them so much that it's like they're still there. That's why I don't think death is so big, cause you'll always be on earth. If one person knows you, you'll always be here.

Encouraging students in our classrooms to participate in discussions that allow them to carve a space for themselves to explore the issues that matter most to them requires a community that can engage in talk that matters to all of the participants—teachers and students.

Creating such a space meant that we were often attempting to operate in the space where tension and community converge. For example, Jay's need to talk about the death of important male figures in his life were juxtaposed with the teacher's need to ensure that students understood the text and the larger inquiry question. In this case, Elizabeth had to allow Jay to talk about his life experiences and use it to better improve his understanding of school content (the text). Although educators often tout that background knowledge is key to comprehension, there often is an unstated understanding that the knowledge we seek to bring to the classroom is a middle class experience. Elizabeth's example countered that image. Instead, what Elizabeth and the rest of us tried to do was to help our students engage in a cyclical process of analyzing how they act on the world and how to reflect on their actions, which we hoped would help them better understand and be more critical of the world, and, by extension, their learning (Freire & Macedo, 1987).

As we attempted to create authentic spaces for our students and ourselves to engage in critical inquiry pedagogy, we realized that a central component of authentic interaction is the ever-shifting component of discourse. In the classroom and in our small cohort, the interactions are less artificial and are primarily centered around the students and our need to know, question, and express one's understanding. The focus on the interaction is not on a particular task, but on the purpose behind the task. In the case of our classrooms, we found that the more we encouraged and supported students' search for genuine understanding, the more social the learning became, which allowed opportunities for the various students voices to be heard. The voices students heard in the classroom were not there to force specific perspectives on other students, but to say things that had to be said. In this space, learning cannot be dictated but must arise out of a true need to understand.

■ Implications for Participants and Other Educators

As we examined our teaching and our interaction with one another, it became clear to us that all discourse is contextualized to a particular space and time, and teachers and students speak language that is affected by multiple conditions. The net effect is that although education can be planned to meet standards and be structured within mandated parameters, its multiple purposes and ranging expectations are not something that teachers can escape by scripting, computerizing, or unifying instruction. Because words do not exist outside of a context, neither does instruction.

Like a novel, the classroom is never hermetically sealed. Instead, within the heteroglossic space of a classroom, centripetal (unifying) and centrifugal (dispersing) forces are always at work. The unifying forces in the classroom include most—but not all—teacher talk, standardization of curriculum and evaluation, and norms of schooling. In the educational tenor of high-stakes testing and paced curricula, teachers and students alike feel the authoritative pressure of unifying forces (i.e., mandated curriculum used for instruction) trying to centralize and normalize education. The intention of policymakers is to unify and standardize education so all students will meet expectations and learn equally well. They pass their edicts to us from on high without any interest in the individual context of the classroom. Yet diversifying forces, such as the goals and expectations of teachers, students, and parents, are always at work. The language of dissent echoes through students who pull disruptive pranks and do not respond well to the stress of standardized tests, through teachers who grouse, and, hopefully, more productively through the voices heard in critical inquiry classrooms. Whether teachers acknowledge centrifugal forces or not, they are ever present because none of our thoughts, words, or actions are without ever-changing contexts, nor can human beings be calcified into ideological statues no matter how strong the centripetal force.

The classroom cannot ignore the give-and-take of these opposing forces. If we structure and stylize our classrooms to only respond to the authoritative expectations of the centripetal forces of policymakers far distant from classrooms, we are ignoring the unique voices of our students and our selves. Critical inquiry pedagogy moves the teacher away from authoritative discourse and closer to something more authentic—internally persuasive discourse, which allows for maximal interaction between a word and its context and a learner and his or her world. When policymakers and administrators give students and teachers space to question, wonder, share, and hypothesize, those students and teachers are more likely to create internally persuasive discourse. Of course, teachers cannot abdicate all authoritative discourse and authoritarian responsibility, nor can they ignore centripetal forces; yet within the heteroglossia of a classroom, teachers will do a great disservice if they expend large amounts of energy suppressing the internally persuasive word (authentic voice) or limiting the centrifugal forces with which we transact. As we—Amanda, Eurydice, Elizabeth, and Ellen—experienced in our classrooms, when we provided opportunities for students to raise risky questions and take more responsibility for their own learning, our voices mingled with a community dedicated to learning that which the state mandated, but also what our hearts dictated.

CHAPTER 4

The Taking of Responsibility One Two Three: Using Critical Inquiry Pedagogy to Take Ownership of Learning

The Stories of Our Questions
The Responsibility Cohort

During this study, Andrea Pintaone-Hernandez was a first-year teacher teaching second grade at South Jackson School, Athens, Georgia, USA; Bob Fecho was a teacher educator at the University of Georgia, Athens; Hope Vaughn moved from teaching language arts at a high school in Washington, Georgia, to teaching a sixth-grade language arts class at Elbert County Middle School, Elberton, Georgia; and Jennifer Aaron was a reading specialist for Chase Elementary in Athens.

Bob Fecho. Bill Cosby (1998), the comedian and actor, once began a comedy album with the line "I started out as a child." If time and space permitted, I could probably trace the genesis of my question back to my own childhood. In many ways, various choices and experiences in my life have colluded to frame a way of looking—a way of making meaning—that relies upon critically inquiring into those choices and experiences. Most recently, as I made the adjustment from being a high school teacher to a teacher educator, I worried about the conflicted world into which I was sending novice teachers to teach. As I saw federal and state policymakers limiting and disrespecting teachers through restrictive curriculum and pervasive testing, I worried that the critical inquiry pedagogy I advocated might get lost in the rush to hold these new teachers accountable.

As a teacher, then and now, for me teaching has always been about taking responsibility for my practice rather than being held accountable by rigid dictates that unseen policymakers write. Teaching and learning are inherently about teachers and learners. The vast network of administrators, curriculum experts, policymakers, university researchers, and the like—of which I am now one—is somewhat of an afterthought. A basic premise for me is that those of us in education who no longer teach in K–12 classrooms have to imagine ourselves less as supervisors and more as advocates of the work done by teachers and learners in classrooms. Those who don't teach need to create educational spaces that support teachers and learners taking responsibility for the work done there. Therefore, in terms of this study, I sought to understand what it means for teachers in any classroom to encourage themselves and their students to take responsibility for their work. In particular, I was interested in the ways novice teachers negotiated these transactions and what support or distraction our small cohort provided.

Hope Vaughn. My first year of teaching and my student teaching experience were in the high school setting. My second year of teaching found me in a new school environment. I was now teaching middle grades. There were many differences between the two. One of the most striking was the emphasis placed on standardized testing. Due to the High School Graduation Test and a recent push toward end-of-course assessments, I was familiar with standardized testing. However, nothing had prepared me for the onslaught of testing I would encounter as a middle grades teacher. As a result of the oversaturation of standardized testing, as well as increasing mandates and pressures to work what some observers might call statistical miracles in terms of performance, I really began to question what the stakeholders in a classroom really wanted, needed, and deserved.

I defined the stakeholders as students, teachers, and administrators. "Administrators" are not limited to the decision-making body of a school or board office. They encompass politicians, business people, government officials, and others who have the power to blindly enforce a one-size-fits-all legislation on people who, in actuality, have quite diverse needs. I then began investigating what my students brought to the learning environment, what they were seeking, and what they were willing to take away from such a setting. I also began questioning my own motives in terms of my selection of classroom materials, as well as my expectations of classroom behavior, participation, and performance. I was then left with this range of questions: Given the relationship of a student and teacher in a learning situation, what is the role of the "administration"? Should they be responsible for determining the curriculum, and, as a result, the assessment of a body of students they did not know? Should the individual student matter in terms of assessment? Could and should learning indeed be simplified and generalized to such a point that nothing of import was really being learned?

This newfound, unfamiliar, and even uncomfortable environment served as a fountain of inquiry. I spent the resulting two years recording instances that stood out to me—I was surprised by the natural, inevitable way my data continued to circle around this question: What happens in that contact zone where students', teachers', and administrators' agendas transact?

Andrea Pintaone-Hernandez. The story of my question cannot be separated from the stories of the questions of the coresearchers in my small cohort. When this project began, I had two very broad questions guiding my inquiry into the literacy learning and community of my second-grade students: (1) In what ways does critical inquiry pedagogy surface across subject matter of an elementary curriculum? and (2) What does this mean for pedagogy in general and how does this transact with issues of multiliteracies? As our small cohort met throughout that first year of the project and we engaged in a reflective process adapted from Carini's descriptive review (in Himley with Carini, 2000), we began to see some common threads in all of our data. It seemed as though we were all noticing the importance of students taking an increased responsibility for their learning.

For me, one of the most difficult aspects of being a first-year teacher was negotiating between allowing my students to become more accountable for their learning and preparing them for state-sanctioned standardized tests, which are given in part to measure my professional accountability. As these issues unfolded in my classroom, my inquiry became guided by the following question: What does inquiry-based teaching and learning mean in helping second-grade students take ownership of their learning and think metacognitively—that is, reflect on their own thought and learning processes about their school experiences? My inquiry became guided by the notion that if my students perceived what they did in our classrooms as relevant to their lives both inside and outside school, then their investment in their own learning—whether to prepare for standardized tests or another objective—would be infinitely more profound.

Jennifer Aaron. My question came about in part because the cohort I was joining was already investigating issues of responsibility in critical inquiry classrooms. How, then, could I take this theme and develop questions that would be pertinent to my students and our classroom circumstance? After all, isn't the point of teacher research to inquire into my own classroom?

My students were involved in an academic service-learning project in which they critically were investigating their school history and for which we ultimately aimed to create a brochure about that history. This, too, tied directly into student responsibility, so I asked, What happens to student responsibility when their school asks them to look at the bigger picture in regard to learning? What does it mean when we focus learning on what can be given back to the community and the student rather than focus solely on isolated academic skills to be rotely learned by students? These questions not only fit into our cohort's theme of responsibility, but they also provided me with a way to look at my students' interactions and reactions, as well as at my own involvement with a way of teaching and learning that they had not been exposed to before.

ra Shor (1992) has spoken to the complexity of classrooms where teachers and students attempt to inquire critically into, as Freire (1983) would say, "the word and the world." In particular, Shor has recognized that, at the least, three agendas operate in all classrooms: (1) the teacher's, (2) the students', and (3) that imposed from the school community writ large. In a teaching journal excerpt, Andrea Pintaone-Hernandez, then a first-year teacher of second grade in a rural school with a predominantly working class, European American student population, expressed her frustration in trying to negotiate these three agendas:

> For instance, last week we (the teachers [in my school district]) were required to give 3 computerized tests to our students (in reading, language arts, and math). When I arrived at the computer lab with my class, we discovered that these tests were extremely difficult to "navigate." It took us nearly an hour just to get everyone [all the students] logged in. By the time the kids actually got to the tests, they were so bored and frustrated that most of them just [chose random answers].
>
> Anyway, my point (I think) is that I am frustrated that "Somebody" in the "district office" is getting to make all the decisions about how I and my students spend our days. Mr. Somebody (and I mean the Mr. in both the literal and figurative senses) doesn't know me OR my students! We certainly don't get to tell anyone in the District Office how to spend their days. They hired us as "professionals," it says so on my teaching certificate, I promise.... They expect us to use "professional judgment" all the time. Well, my "professional judgment" tells me that no one knows better than my students and me how we should spend our days....

In this excerpt, Andrea feels constrained by the district office's decisions about testing. By taking her students to the computer lab and helping them negotiate the complexities of this testing procedure, she demonstrates a need to support these decisions and help her students get through such tasks successfully. For their part, students go through the expectations and rituals set for them by the adults in their life, yet often they feel equally frustrated and disengaged from these tasks. And, we—Andrea, Bob Fecho, Hope Vaughn, and Jennifer Aaron—argue that no one, in the end, feels happy about the results of such anonymous, alienating teaching-and-learning decisions, not even the disembodied and often patriarchal voice of district personnel, who seem to have the advantage in this situation.

It is our belief that policies that inflict too much rigidity into curriculum and assessment and that do so from a distance set up an atmosphere where frustration is rampant (Schultz & Fecho, 2005). Connecting to our earlier discussion of Bakhtin (1981), we worry that such policy creates too much centripetal tendency, and that district policymakers skew the learning community far past stabilization to a point of petrifaction. Teachers sense that their hands are tied in making substantive classroom decisions; students chafe under curricula, pedagogy, and assessment that remove them from making connections to their lives; and even sensitive district office personnel intuit that their efforts are not garnering real support within schools.

By mandating teaching practice from a distance—a distance that is both spatial and temporal—and then holding teachers and students, although rarely themselves, accountable for the learning that results from those decisions, administrators and policymakers create conditions under which scores on testing might improve, but little occurs in the way of substantive and critical learning (Kohn, 2000; Murphy, 1998). Students might test well, but they still struggle as meaning makers, as citizens in a democracy who can interpret and compose complicated text concerning complicated issues in the increasingly complicated world emerging in the 21st century (New London Group, 2000).

We don't argue, however, for an elimination of outside agendas from classrooms, as if that were actually possible. Instead, we argue for a different kind of relationship among teachers, students, and administration. Teaching began as a transaction between teachers and students. Before curriculum supervisors, principals, teacher educators, secretaries of education, or federal regulators existed, education was the purview of teachers and students coming together to learn. In order for transactions that lead to substantive and critical meaning to occur between teachers and students, those of us with the power to do so—the voting public, policymakers, teacher educators and the like—need to create ways for teachers and students to take more responsibility for what occurs in classrooms. Those who no longer inhabit K–12 classrooms need to be less supervisory and more facilitative. Rather than holding teachers and students accountable—an othering if we ever saw one—those who are no longer teachers or students need to enter into a dialogue with them that will create conditions that permit teachers and students to take responsibility for what occurs in classrooms.

In this chapter, we show, through four cases researched within our small cohort and in our own critical inquiry classrooms, what it might look like for teachers and students to take responsibility for their learning, what complications might arise, and what efforts might be made to transcend such complications. We also hope to bring a personal face to such work to remind us all that education is only partly about percentiles and publishable scores, but, more importantly, is about substantive daily transactions in the lives of learners that lead, as Dewey suggests (1938), to multiple and ever increasingly more worthwhile learning experiences.

■ Not Your Father's Sense of Responsibility: Teachers and Students Taking Ownership in the Classroom

In concert with the ideas we just expressed, we want to complicate the concept of *responsibility*. In particular, we don't want to be seen as refreshing the old "pull yourself up by your bootstraps" argument, that all it takes for students to succeed academically, particularly those who are disenfranchised, is to stop complaining about how bad things are and to go out and get what is needed. As teachers who have all taught marginalized student populations, we are too aware that although we encourage students to be proactive in their lives, not all of our students, due largely to social status coupled to socially constructed power issues, have the same access to options and possibilities that enable such "self-actualizing" activities. So although we don't condone whining about one's lot in life, we also don't condone the denial of critical inequities that most certainly exist and that continue to favor populations whose discourse more clearly matches that of the dominant population.

To convey what we mean by *taking responsibility*, we find it more appropriate to offer this excerpt from a draft written by Hope:

> As a teacher who often feels very [confused, even] out of control, within my own [teaching] practice, the word *responsibility* makes me somewhat uncomfortable. I think that it is one of those words that conveys traits such as trust, authority, a commanding presence, and a controlled and organized manner. I don't have a problem with any of these elements; however, I don't always feel that I exhibit such characteristics. So when pondering what it means to take responsibility for myself as a teacher, I run into a brick wall of jargon. What I have to do is adopt a definition of responsibility that I can embrace and exemplify. While I think there are very old-school ideas associated with *responsibility*, I also think that there are basic assumptions that go along nicely with the term. I think that a teacher who takes responsibility for herself is taking ownership of learning, being accountable for the content and assessment of her course, and making herself an interactive part of the teacher-and-student relationship. If I think of responsibility in this light—as a way of being more student centered and less teacher centered—then I can visualize ways in which I have often taken responsibility

for myself as teacher and learner. I can also see ways in which students have been enabled to become responsible learners.

In order for students and teachers to take responsibility for, or as Hope puts it, take ownership of, the learning occurring in their classroom, they must rethink relationships and engender those relationships that create opportunities for all teachers and students to embrace the possibilities for making meaning that come with intentional inquiries into language.

So in asking students and teachers to take more responsibility for learning, we are not asking them to go it alone, to just hunker down and get on with it as the rest of society blissfully ignores them, that is, until there is some political hell to pay. Instead, we argue that dialogue must occur among all educational stakeholders that facilitates and supports in all ways the taking of responsibility by those most directly affected by the outcomes. Those that do must have more say in how, why, and when things get done. With ownership comes the responsibility to do what feels most appropriate and critical to the learning that occurs.

■ Portraits of the Taking of Responsibility: What Taking Responsibility Means for Teachers and Students

In writing about her classroom, Jennifer noted that according to Gustavsen (2001), critical inquiry "can inform a process of enlightenment and out of this process can emerge new practices" (p. 18), which can help students and teachers to see the connections between the school world and the world outside of school. In order for teachers and students to take responsibility, new practices and relationships must occur, both within the classroom and outwardly from that classroom, among a range of stakeholders. In the following four cases, we give examples of how such relationships can form, what is complicated about such a construction, and what it might mean for such a construction to occur.

Bob's Classroom: Exploring the Use of Inquiry and Reading in the Content Areas

As a former high school teacher and now a teacher educator, I have been exploring the process of critical inquiry for over 15 years. Although my experience has taught me to trust that process, there are still those nettlesome moments, usually midsemester, when I'm just not sure that all class participants are embracing my expectation (that students will make meaning for themselves). This concern was brought home clearly to me as I worked with a group of middle school preservice teachers—mostly European American middle class women in their third year at a university —in a course designed to help content area teachers imagine using reading in their classrooms. In particular, a group of students whose major content concentration was mathematics seemed to struggle particularly with the possibilities of inquiry as a viable classroom strategy. In addition to raising concerns about their own classrooms, they often wondered if they were gaining anything of use as I modeled that mode of teaching.

Having taught this course several times in the past, I had come to see that mathematics majors generally were most resistant to ideas of using reading in their classroom, especially from a critical inquiry perspective. With this experience in mind, I had asked four preservice teachers in the mathematics concentration to communicate weekly with me via e-mail to share how they were making meaning of the class and what concerns they might be encountering. In addition, I asked permission to take notes on their classroom discussions, keep copies of their work for close analysis, and interview them when the course had ended. While these students were writing to me about their reactions to the class, I was writing on a weekly basis to Andrea, Hope, and Jennifer about my own reactions to what had occurred in the classroom.

Of these students, Hayley stood out for a number of reasons. For one, she was the most consistent in her weekly writing. In addition, she seemed to register a range of responses about the class and did so with a detail that was illuminating. From week to week, I could count on her to respond openly and candidly both in class and by e-mail.

However, despite a general appreciation for my efforts, Hayley began to express concerns about the direction of the class, wondering if the focus on inquiry was relevant for her future classroom. In response to our ninth session, she began her weekly reaction somewhat ominously with, "I have strong feelings about today, and I just hope that anything that I say will not affect my grade or your thoughts about me. I am simply trying to express how I felt." In writing to Andrea, Jennifer, and Hope, I began my own reaction to the session with similar foreboding: "I'm somewhat ambivalent about this session, especially my role." It seems evident from both our opening statements that our mutual exploration into inquiry and reading had gone somewhat awry.

After these somewhat negative e-mail beginnings, Hayley and I went on to express what seemed to have gone well for us. Knowing how a cadre of mathematics majors, including Hayley, was struggling with inquiry-based pedagogy, I had mentioned my experience at an ethnography conference session where mental mathematics activities were posited to help students inquire into number relationships. This was followed by a look at narrative data from my own high school classes in which students examined the complexities of making meaning for themselves. The discussions that came out of this work were lively and fired with emotion. Hayley seemed to agree. In her reaction, she followed her opening caveat by expressing, "Today was interesting. I enjoyed the class in the fact that I got really passionate about what we were discussing and what we were talking about and my own opinions."

Yet we both agreed that at some point what I had intended to be dialogue, a sharing of views with an intent to learn from all perspectives, had shifted into debate, an arguing for one view to be "right." Near the end of our discussion, it seemed to me that Hayley and two other mathematics majors had dug their trench against inquiry and were no longer entertaining other perspectives. I wrote to my cohort:

> I got a bit frustrated because [this group of three students] kept going back to issues of coverage, standardized tests, and quantitative research methods as arguments against inquiry. I found myself arguing for inquiry because I felt that [they] were often ignoring evidence that was present in class or were privileging some data over others. So in the end, I wondered if I was pushing my agenda too hard. I did mention that my intent was not to make them inquiry teachers, that if they did not believe [in inquiry] they should not use it, but that I did want them to have a clear grasp of why they felt as they did.

I have previously experienced this feeling of impasse before with other classes. At some point, I find myself arguing for a viewpoint and, in that arguing, I can feel the students sealing themselves off, refusing to hear what I so desperately want them to hear.

> I'm well aware of the irony at work in the situation I have just described. I believe in a classroom where multiple perspectives can and should be supported, so I have to imagine students who will not embrace inquiry as pedagogy. I'm fully prepared to do that in theory and largely prepared to

implement that in action. However, what bothered me most about this resistance is that I hadn't felt that it was hard won. It was my sense that this small but insistent group of students was dismissing out of hand rather than basing their concerns upon some purposeful inquiry of intent. When I found myself arguing, it was mainly to push them to consider some other perspectives and to bring more focus to their concerns.

On the other hand, Hayley largely felt attacked. In her words from her weekly reaction, the session was

> too much a sparring match...and it really frustrated me today when it was a boxing match about who was right instead of a calm devil's advocate. There are no right or wrong answers...I am sorry if I seem rude, but I am not trying to be. I just felt things got out of hand today and we were being ridiculed for having doubts about using inquiry-based learning in all aspects of our teaching.

The very passionate discussion that Hayley praised at the start of her response was more than what she wanted to contend with, to the point where she found herself calling for someone, presumably me, to play a more dispassionate devil's advocate role. At base, the discussion had come a bit too close to her personal comfort zone, and her preference was for an activity that would grant some emotional distance.

In closing, Hayley offered both portent and insight for my understanding of where our work might need to go in order to move beyond this impasse. She wrote:

> Also I am concerned about how to teach reading. I do not really feel that I have a lot of information that I will walk away with about how to teach it. The activities are useful, and so are the readings, but it seems we are so involved with learning about inquiry-based learning that I am not getting what I feel is important to me.

From my stance, Hayley wasn't seeing the classroom for the desks. But she was expressing her needs and calling out for some metacognitive activity that would help pull the experience of the previous nine weeks into focus, particularly for reading in the content area.

I started my reaction to the next session with, "My goodness. I'm exhausted," an evaluation of how I exited that class, and followed this with a sense of how I had entered:

> I went into class worried. As I had written about last week and as some
> e-mail from my students confirmed, I sensed that perhaps I had pushed
> on inquiry too hard, that the discussion had lapsed into debate and was
> no longer dialogue. Some mathematics students in particular...seemed to
> be digging in on their stances rather than opening them to inquiry. And I
> had followed them, sort of unrelentingly trying to make my points. So I
> went into class feeling I had to mend fences. Not to apologize necessarily,
> but to try and steer our group interaction back to dialogue. I acknowledged
> the need to mend fences in class.

Although I suspected, and subsequent interviews confirmed, that the concerns that were very large to some of us were little more than a blip on the radar screen to most others, I felt it important that Hayley's comments and my own observations not go unnoticed or unconsidered. From my perspective, the issues raised by Hayley and her peers were integral to the course because, as we will show, they opened up the course to the kind of in-depth understanding that those of us in class were seeking.

It is odd that for a class built on critical inquiry, I took a teacher-centered stance to start our 10th session. I felt it important to remind them about the paths we had taken and what understandings we had come to along the way. In particular, I pulled out and reshared information from overhead transparencies the class had generated about the importance of reading and what made for good literacy instruction. I then put up the first of five class-generated overheads on inquiry-based instruction. The first one showed the assumptions about teaching and learning that were evident in an inquiry-based classroom. The second one showed the disadvantages of inquiry, and I indicated points on this table that I disagreed with (e.g., cannot cover standards), points I agreed with (e.g., critical inquiry is time-consuming), and even points I had added to the list (e.g., critical inquiry can be threatening). We continued to discuss advantages, structures, and processes that support inquiry, and structures and processes that do not support inquiry. All the while, my intent was to help the students see that we had generated a menu about issues in the class and that they could choose what they believed from that menu, as long as they interrogated their thinking on those issues.

Knowing Hayley's concern about not seeing a connection to reading in her content area, I then asked the class to respond to the following prompt: What does teaching from an inquiry stance have to do with reading in content areas? As the class started writing on this question, I sat off to the side of the classroom particularly watching Hayley because this activity was in response to her expressed needs. I watched as she stared down at her pad, her pen poised, but eliciting no movement. She sighed, relaxed, poised again, did a false start, and once more relaxed. She looked across at another mathematics major who was also having trouble getting started. Looking up, she caught my eye observing her and asked, "This may seem like a stupid question, but I need to know what teaching reading in the content area is before I can answer this question."

At last the question was out. It had taken 10 sessions, but the question had finally come up through Hayley's insistence and frustration. As I wrote in my reaction, I found myself transported back in time to my high school class. Almost every year near midpoint some student would ask, "How is this [engaging in inquiry projects] English?" As a younger teacher, I was just flabbergasted and made defensive by such a question. But I had come to trust inquiry. So I would just ask the class, "How is this English?" and we would brainstorm and come away with a greater metacognitive understanding of the class.

Falling back on that experience, I asked, "What does it mean to teach reading in the content areas?" Sparked by this question, a lively discussion occurred with many students offering their views and expressing a range of ideas based upon readings and discussions we had had previously. In addition, another student raised a concern about struggling readers, and again, I guided the class to use the work we had done together to bear upon that question. Slowly, but with authority, the class brainstormed eight suggestions for helping struggling readers, again from our prior course experience.

Hayley's response to class was one of her more succinct ones but also one that was quite revealing. She wrote:

> Well, I don't have much to say about today's class since I said so much in class, but I do have to say thank you for showing us that we have been learning to teach reading. I guess it's like the whole concept people have that if they aren't reading a book, they are not reading. We just felt that because we weren't being lectured at or talking in an obvious, direct way about the topic, that we weren't getting what we were supposed to. I think today's discussion went really well, and I really felt like I got a lot out of it. It was, I guess, the kind of open class ("inquiry-based learning") that I would do in my classroom. It is important that you are interested in what we think and where we are, otherwise your whole theory would be shot.

Although I have no illusions that this experience was enough to suddenly turn Hayley into an inquiry-based teacher, one who consistently and intently used inquiry in her classes and as a means for understanding her classes, I am convinced that this experience, combined with other similar experiences, will yield that result. It was not my main intention necessarily to turn Hayley into an inquiry-based teacher, although I would have looked upon such an occurrence with satisfaction. What I did want was an intelligent and informed investigation, brief as it might be, into what it means to take a critical inquiry stance on a classroom and an experience with such a stance, one that might reveal through action what might remain tacit in a dispassionate discussion. My belief, as evidenced by the circumstances of these two sessions, is that I got what I wanted. My hope is that such an experience primed Hayley for future experiences that would deepen her understanding of such classroom work.

Like Bob, Hope also was experiencing challenges from students regarding the disparities between how they were used to learning and what they were now experiencing in her classroom. Again, the questions arise of what counts as learning in an English classroom and what it means for students and teachers to coconstruct responsibility for the learning that occurs there.

Hope's Classroom: Sharing Authority With Students to "Do English"

This portrait was born of a disgruntled class of high school students. It was my first year teaching, and I was tired and felt that I had been doing all the work in the classroom. I was feeling unappreciated. Students were overwhelmed by how different this classroom was being taught than previous ones. They really were convinced that I didn't know what I was doing. After all, where were the isolated grammar lessons, weekly vocabulary quizzes, end-of-chapter tests—for that matter, where was the textbook? They were unable to connect what we were doing in class to what "doing" school had looked like in the past. Discussions, writing, and projects didn't connect to what students felt they should be experiencing daily in the classroom. They challenged me to offer them evidence that our classroom practices were legitimate forms of learning.

Jake: We don't do nothin' in here.
Ronald: Yeah. Nothin'.

Hope:	What do you mean?
Jake:	I mean, we don't do nothin' in here. What class is this anyway?
Hope:	English.
Ronald:	Man, I am goin' to fail the end of course test because you ain't teachin' me anything.
Hope:	What do you usually do in an English classroom?
Jake:	Read literature, answer the questions.
Ronald:	Yeah. You supposed to be teachin' me how to talk right. You know, grammar and stuff.
Hope:	Oh...
Jake:	All we ever do in here is talk. I mean we write and stuff, but it's not really English.

I was taken back to a previous conversation with a student in which she commented, "When are we going to start doing English...you know, book work?" Again, this incongruence between how an English classroom traditionally functions and how it might function stunned me. I began to wonder if we really were "doing English." I looked at the breakdown of the course. It was divided into five nationally recognized strands: (1) reading, (2) writing, (3) speaking, (4) listening, and (5) viewing. I thought,

> We do these. We read. Lots of stuff. Lots of genres—I try to find relevant materials—we go beyond the canon. We write—so much so that they complain. We do not write five-paragraph essays, just words—as many as possible. We certainly speak; no one in here is shy. Probably 60% of our class time is used for speaking. We definitely need to work on listening. There are plenty of opportunities to listen, but we do not use them well. What about viewing? We watch documentaries, evaluate art, and the like, but we do not call it viewing. Overall, I think we are meeting the goals of an English classroom, so where is the chasm between what I see us doing and their perceptions?

I wanted to blame the students. After all, they were failing to see the opportunities before them. Holding off on blaming them overtly, I began to look at the issue of trust. All of their comments echoed that same sentiment, "We do not recognize what you are doing. We do not know you, therefore, we do not trust you." I realized that while I had given them no reason to distrust me, I still must earn their trust. Yet, even with this new realization, I continued to be frustrated by their comments.

As the *teacher*, I felt some amount of respect, participation, and attention should be inherent to my position. Why couldn't they do what I was asking them simply because I was the *teacher* and I had asked them to do so? Why didn't they come in, sit quietly, and raise their hands just because that is what an orderly contributing member of society does? This is when it dawned on me that I was not their *teacher*, at least not in the sense that any of their or my own past perceptions and experiences had defined.

I was confused. I wanted a quiet, productive classroom. Yet many classrooms I'd had firsthand experience with had been quiet but often not productive. I wanted to have discussions, do projects, and change the world. But most of the teaching models I had seen had only involved taking roll, giving an assignment, and grading tests. I had to change my perception of what the classroom should look like and of what my role and the students' role should be in such a classroom. This was painful, uncomfortable, and constantly evolving. It was hard to admit that I was being inconsistent. I was trying to enforce the environment that I was used to in school but attempting to "teach" in an innovative way. I wanted students to be engaged and productive, but quiet, seated, and attentive to my cue. I was not really sharing responsibility for learning with my students.

Seeing that I was drained and disheartened, the principal intervened. He spent a day in my room holding Open-Mike Friday. Given this opportunity to air their concerns and opinions about any topic they wished, my students lined up for the chance. Just as I was relishing how nice this break was going to be, Ronald spoke up. "I want to talk about this class." My stomach sank. The scowl on his face said all I needed to know about the message that would follow. In the next five minutes, students called me a hypocrite, a promise breaker, and accused me of everything short of mass murder, unless you count purposely attempting to fail a class of students. I was crying profusely, and here was the principal turning what I saw as an attack against me into this lesson of personal responsibility, respect, and survival.

This ensued throughout the day. I could not focus, had no confidence on the floor, and was praying for the day to end. When I did finally leave school, I was grateful to the principal for bailing me out, but feared what might be the repercussions of "not fighting my own battles," as one student put it. I spent the weekend convinced that inquiry and student-centered classrooms were an ideal only for the college classroom and that on Monday morning I would begin book work. It's what the students wanted, wasn't it?

The following Monday, I laid books on desktops, wrote assignments on the board, and went over the new and appropriately rigid rules for class. I was ready to be the teacher they expected. However, Michael had something quite different in mind. He raised his hand requesting permission to speak to me after class. I asked him if his question had to do with class. I encouraged him to bring it before the whole class if it did. I think I was imagining another personal attack and was ready to come out swinging. A few students were aware of what he had to say, and they convinced him to share with the class. There I was: depressed, defensive, and tired—and all of a sudden "out of the mouths of babes" came the answer we had all been searching for.

Michael: Well, Mrs. V., I was just wondering if we could do some kind of video project for the community.

Hope: What did you have in mind?

Michael: Ummm. I was thinking we could record the football games and show them on Channel 54 for people who don't have transportation to the games.

Hope: OK. What purpose would that serve?

Michael: Well, a lot of people can't go to games, and students don't ever take a role in the community. This would be a chance to bring the school to the community and all.

Hope: How would we do this?

These questions and answers went on for an entire class session. Other students were sharing their opinions, and we never opened our literature book. By the end of class, we had downsized our project into a possible task and began making plans for the next day—students were actually taking an interest in and responsibility for what we would need to do in order to make this happen. It was contagious.

Now I was seeing the engagement and effort I had craved from students. They were connecting work they did in school with the idea of meaningful and authentic work in the community. English was becoming very real and very useful to this class. Particularly, my students were seeing ways for learning about reading, writing, speaking, listening, and viewing that weren't directly connected to skill-and-drill methods (rote means of learning in which one is introduced to a concept and then practices it repeatedly until it is absorbed for immediate regurgitation), but that would yield quality learning experiences through their execution in the context of an engaging community-based project. In planning for and producing these videos, students would solve problems; research, read, and produce complicated text; collaborate; and offer critique in a variety of language codes that represented ways of communicating and expressing identity at home, among peers, and in academic settings. We would very much be doing English.

This occurred because one student took the initiative and responsibility for his learning and because I took responsibility for supporting learning in any way that they could embrace. We definitely became colearners in this process. They taught me as much as I taught them.

Finally, I was understanding what classroom responsibility might mean for myself and my students. I was sharing the authority of the classroom with my students, and students were hearing my voice as a contributor instead of a controller—a contributor whose input was necessary, valuable, and sought after. Because there was an authentic task at hand, students talked, but at tolerable noise levels; they moved about the room, but with a purpose; they asked questions that we all worked to answer using the tools of reading, writing, speaking, listening, and viewing. They requested my help but were learning about all the tools to help themselves. We, both teacher and students, were embracing learning in a manner reminiscent of Wilhelm (1997) when he wrote, "By combining our various voices, perhaps we can devise a map and a sense of the landscape that will help us all to become better and more independent readers of words and, as Freire encourages us, readers of the world" (p. 9). As a teacher, I want nothing more than to provide a classroom that welcomes such "various voices" and offers opportunities for learning that students will embrace as meaningful for that moment, yet as empowering for their lives.

In another case in which the teacher and student become colearners, Andrea describes how she and one of her students learned to take ownership of their learning in the classroom. As Andrea struggled as both a novice teacher and researcher, she learned to trust not only the inquiry process but also a student's need to take ownership of her learning.

Andrea's Classroom: Taking Responsibility Through Self-Assessment

My teaching context for the data-gathering portion of this study took place in a second-grade classroom in a rural, suburban elementary school located just outside of Athens, Georgia, USA. It was my first year of teaching. When the school year began, two broad questions guided my critical inquiry: (1) How does critical inquiry surface across subject matter of an elementary curriculum? and (2) How do critical inquiry pedagogy issues transact with multiliteracies? The primary source of data was my teaching journal. My first journal entries, in retrospect, sound to me like nothing more than complaining, but they evolved into a place where I began to make sense of the "big picture"—how my classroom worked within the larger systems of the school, the district, and society. I began to understand how taking a critical inquiry stance in my classroom challenged my students and me to take an increased sense of responsibility for our learning.

When I started my teaching career and collecting data, I used my weekly journal entries at first as a place to air my frustration and exhaustion about teaching. Looking back, I noticed that my journal entries during the months of September, October, and November are rife with the ramblings of a struggling first-year teacher. It is clear from my teaching journal that as the school year began, I was indeed overwhelmed with my daily roles and responsibilities as a second-grade teacher. A recurring theme in these entries is frustration. Specifically, a large disconnect existed between how I perceived the organization of my classroom curriculum and assessment and the realities of standardized tests.

As the year continued, I focused my data collection, and thus my journal entries, on one student, Zaria, an African American girl whose academic work was far above second-grade level. I chose to focus my observations and reflections on her in my first attempt to describe the range of students' responses I saw in my classroom to inquiry-based teaching and learning and to student self-assessment. Zaria was motivated by the challenge of setting her own learning goals and taking responsibility for them. I wrote the following in my journal:

> I picked [this] student because I find myself talking about [her] the most both with other teachers and with people outside of school. I identify with [her] on many levels—and so that is most likely why I feel a connection with [her]. Zaria and I have strong grandmothers who have played central roles in our upbringings. As learners, we both have a need to question everything—sometimes to a fault. Zaria is the kind of student every first-year teacher hopes to have: responsible, honest, intelligent, and helpful.

The questions initially guiding my inquiry also evolved as the group met and analyzed parts of my journal. My research then became driven by the following question: What does inquiry-based teaching and learning mean when a teacher helps a second-grade student take responsibility for her learning and her metacognitition about her school experiences? By choosing to focus on an individual student and revising my inquiry questions, I saw how issues related to assessment and how responsibility permeated the data.

I used this knowledge to rethink parts of my classroom. During the second half of the school year, I planned for my students take a more active role in the assessment and evaluation of their learning. To do this, each student made a weekly list of learning goals in reading, writing, and mathematics. During one-on-one conferences with students, as well as during whole-group instruction, I referred to students' specific goals. For example, during a writing conference with an individual student, I might say something such as, "How does this story you have written demonstrate that you are working on your writing goal of wanting to use capital letters in your stories?" This *explicit* goal-setting process seemed to be essential for my students to take an increased sense of responsibility for their learning. In particular, Zaria, my focus student, thrived on the challenge this kind of inquiry-based learning I provided. I wrote in my journal:

> On Wednesday during writing workshop, Zaria handed me a story that she wanted to conference with me about. When I asked her to read it to me, she and I both knew that this wasn't her best work, and she had certainly not put her best effort into it. I referred to her learning goals and asked her how this story helped her reach toward her goal of writing stories that had a beginning, middle, and end. Without saying anything to me, she stood up and went back to her seat to continue working on her draft.

Any teacher would be elated to see a student make that connection between the goals she had set for herself and the daily work she did in class. It was clear to me that by making this change in my classroom, at least some students were indeed taking increased responsibility for their learning.

With some scaffolding, my inquiry stance allowed students to determine and assess their own learning goals. I wrote in my journal:

> I really enjoy this new way of doing "assessment." I like that students get to tell me what they want to learn about, as well as what they feel their strongest qualities are as students and what they feel they need to work on. I have found that my students are their own toughest critics—and their own best teachers. At the end of the three-week grading period, I will ask

each child to reflect on each of the goals they had set for themselves and, based on that, to rewrite, define, and assess their goals for the next grading period.

The individual goal-setting activity seemed to help my students become more aware of their responsibility for their learning in our classroom. I noticed that class discussions became livelier as students looked to one another for support rather than always seeking my assistance.

During the month of February, I read the book *Tar Beach* (Ringgold, 1991) to the class. Zaria was so intrigued by the story that she checked out two of Ringgold's other titles from the library the next day. After reading the books, Zaria asked me if she could read another of Ringgold's books— *Aunt Harriet's Underground Railroad in the Sky* (1992), which extends the story from *Tar Beach*—to the class. I agreed. After the story, I asked my students if they believed the underground railroad was a real train with a conductor, a caboose, and secret railroad tracks. Everyone said they believed the underground railroad was a real train. When I explained that the term *railroad* was symbolic and metaphorical rather than literal, no one believed me, least of all Zaria. Later, she asked me if she could read more about Harriet Tubman and the underground railroad and do a presentation about it at the end of the week. After a bit of hesitation, I agreed to Zaria's self-directed inquiry. When Zaria did present what she had learned, her project was admirable. In my journal, I wrote:

> Zaria decided to start [her inquiry project] by reading the picture book version of Harriet Tubman's biography. Then she talked with her grandmother and preacher about what they knew about Harriet Tubman and the underground railroad. Fortunately they were able to convince her that the [underground] railroad really was a network of people, not an actual railroad. She presented her learning by (a) creating a poster to display in the classroom and (b) performing a speech she had written with herself as Harriet Tubman. It was phenomenal! I am so excited to see her energy and love for the challenges of learning. Holt (1982) pointed out, "A child is most intelligent when the reality before him arouses in him a high degree of attention, interest, concentration, involvement—in short, when he cares most about what he is doing" (p. 265). As a teacher during my first year, I struggled with the pressures to conform my classroom to meet curriculum mandates imposed by outsiders such as politicians and school administrators, while trying to motivate and inspire my students with a love of learning. I suspect many teachers, both novice and veteran, struggle with these issues.

Engaging in this work helped keep me accountable for my own teaching and learning throughout the year, and thus it kept me more in sync with the needs and interests of my students. Reflecting on daily events—or "musings," as our cohort called them—in my teaching journal helped me to understand how my work in this inquiry project was parallel to the ways in which I saw Zaria taking ownership of her learning. In many ways, my teaching journal was the goal sheet I had asked my students to keep, a place where I recorded my teaching and learning goals and objectives, described my strengths and weaknesses as a teacher, and made a plan for my work. By encouraging Zaria to set her own learning goals and evaluate her progress toward reaching them, she saw clearly that *she* was, in fact, her own best teacher.

In another instance of a teacher and students assuming increased ownership of their learning, Jennifer's class entered into an inquiry project to investigate their school history. This academic service-learning project helped Jennifer's fifth-grade students imagine the connections between their classroom and the outside world, and encouraged them to become active citizens in their community.

Jennifer's Classroom: Facilitating Ownership via Academic Service Learning

In a small room in an urban elementary school in Athens sat 11 fifth-grade students at their desks, with their eyes sparkling and hands waving, and wanting to be called upon when the reporter from the local newspaper posed her next question: How did you all get started on this project? There it was—out there. What were they going to say? Ametra led off the conversation:

> We had started 'cause we was talking about, like, when was it? September 11[, 2001]—when the planes had crashed into the Twin Buildings [the Twin Towers of the World Trade Center]. And we were thinking about going on a field trip, and we had, we were going on a field trip to, probably like, what's it called? The funeral home.

The funeral home? What was she talking about? We had never even talked about a funeral home! What was I doing? After all this time, they did not have a clue, but she continued:

> And some kids had got some, they had made up some money for two new fire trucks and.... We were thinking about stuff and making a garden for

the—the shelter. And wasn't it Patrice that said, "Let's...do something about our school?"

Maybe they *were* learning, taking it all in, feeling like they were part of something.

Having recently learned about academic service learning, I introduced it to these students from diverse backgrounds in the hope that they would (a) see the connection between school learning and the "real world" everyone is always referring to and (b) recognize the importance of becoming active citizens, both of the community in which they live as well as in the smaller community of our classroom. *Academic service learning* is a way of teaching that asks students to identify a need in the community, develop a plan that addresses this need, intentionally integrate their academic subjects into the plan, and act out that plan—all while observing and reflecting. In essence, academic service learning engages the students in their own critical action research project. I also was using this opportunity to learn about my own practice and my students' learning within this framework. The process began with my own and the students' written guiding questions. While their questions focused on the goal of the project (e.g., How has the school changed since it was built 80 years ago?), my questions focused on student learning (e.g., What happens to student responsibility when teachers and students are asked to look at the bigger picture in regard to learning? What does it mean when learning focuses on what can be given back to the community and the student, rather than focusing solely on isolated academic skills?).

Teaching is a mix of good and bad days and easy and tremendously difficult moments. Add the expectations of critical inquiry into this mix and imagine the possibilities. *Webster's Ninth New Collegiate Dictionary* (1988) defines *responsibility* as being "able to answer for one's conduct and obligations" (p. 1005); however, this plays out differently in the classroom. As the *teacher*, I see it as my responsibility to provide opportunities for students to share their voices, to teach in a way that is engaging and open to their ideas and suggestions while still focusing my teaching on the state standards, and to be open and honest about what I know and what I don't know. I also know what I consider to be their responsibility— to inquire into things they really want to know about, not just what they think I want them to know. Kenneth's (a student's) question during a discussion of desegregation and the *Brown v. Board of Education* (1954) ruling—"Were the Browns white?"—is an example of just that—engaging in learning; sharing ideas, even if it's risky; and being open to different ways of "doing school." There also is a responsibility of all involved to work toward building a "community of learners" in which none of us has all the answers and, therefore, each has things to learn from one another. With this agenda understood, the students and I started work on this project.

Together, the class and I collected data—we conducted interviews, looked through old school photograph albums, watched films on the decades the school has been in operation, read historical fiction that were set during those same decades, conversed about the project, reflected on efforts that were going well within the project and those things that needed changing, and various other data generated by the class—and began the process of analyzing it.

One of the first things the class did was develop fliers asking anyone who attended or worked at the school and who was interested in sharing their experiences with us to call us. Several people responded. The interviews were the ultimate test; the students were able to articulate the ideas for the project during class discussions and with interested teachers, administrators, and parents, but could they do so with complete strangers? The following is a portion of my journal reflecting on the first interview. The interviewee was a retired teacher who had taught at the school in the early 1970s and was used to being with children.

> The interview started as I had expected. Just kept thinking "let the students do the right thing, *please*!" Carla sounded very strong with her introduction of the project. The students sat quietly; they all seemed to be paying attention to who is supposed to be asking the next question. They seemed to be listening. When they were done asking questions, I asked if there were other questions anyone had thought of...there was this moment of silence, probably less than 30 seconds, but it seemed to last a while. Then suddenly, they started asking their own questions. They were raising their hands waiting to be called on and listening—*wow*! This went on for another 15 minutes. Then we offered the interviewee cookies and a drink and thanked her for coming.
>
> As the students were getting ready to leave for the day, I told them to place their questions and any notes they had taken on their desks. After they left, I started to pick up their notes and I could have cried. They had taken notes—and had not written just "yes" or "no" next to the questions. Two students had been writing narratives as the interviewee answered. The interview lasted about an hour, and not only had they sat quietly for that time, they had paid enough attention to take detailed notes. *Floored! Amazed! Happy dance!* (Picture a white girl doing a subdued Snoopy dance.)

At the time of the newspaper interview, we had been working on this project for two months. I was in awe of how they had taken ownership of this work. *I* had imposed the idea of academic service learning, *I* had suggested that we "do something about our school," *I* planned the activities around which the learning would take place, and yet *the students* were working together to build a "coconstruction of institutional history of the project, creating a mythology of its beginning" (Bob Fecho, personal communication, January 30, 2003). The students amazed me with the knowledge that they seemed to be gaining from this experience, yet at the same time, they frustrated me with questions such as, "When are we going to do the workbook?" How could they not see the benefit of what we were doing? How could they not see that they were part of learning something bigger than "the workbook" could offer them? Yet the issue of responsibility and ownership continued to bother me.

One Monday morning, like so many other Monday mornings I spent with these students, I turned on the computer and SMART Board—a digitally sensitive white board that can be connected to input and output devices—and in response to all my questions and conversation starters, all I got back were these blank stares from the students. This Monday morning hit me differently. We had been working on the history of our school for about five months, and we had been working on this particular section of the brochure for about an hour. It was longer than I had originally thought we would be working on the history of the school, but for the most part, they continued to be enthusiastic and seemed to like being part of learning something special and out of the ordinary. This morning, however, I had had enough of forming thoughts out of students' half-coherent mumbles that I obtained through blatant force, so I sat down in a chair in the corner and said, "If you all will not work with me, I'm not going to stand here and talk to myself. We need to get this section finished up, and you won't go to music until it gets done." It was immature and an easy way out, but it was effective. After about two minutes of silence and questioning looks, a few hands went up. "I'm not helping you. You need to work together to figure this out; I'm only staying because there has to be an adult in the room."

Another two minutes of silence passed. Was I going to have to relent and take charge in spite of my better judgment? Then Kenneth stood up, walked over to the board, and asked the class if he could make a change to the second sentence. They agreed. Carla went up next. Slowly, instead of me, they began to take charge; it was amazing. They were not only working together to accomplish a task, but they were being respectful of one another's thoughts and ideas. Needless to say, they went to music on time. When I returned to my room, on my chair was a letter from the class, written in friendly letter format (a Georgia Language Arts standard), apologizing for their lack of involvement at the beginning of class and asking that I please come back and be their teacher. Here they were using state curriculum in real and practical ways. When they returned from music, they seemed energized. I had decided in their absence that what happened would have to be discussed. I needed them to know I was proud and impressed with what they had accomplished on their own, but at the same time, it should not have come about the way it did.

One of the goals of public schools has always been to educate thoughtful, active citizens who are able to make connections to "real-life" circumstances (Dewey, 1916). Research (National Commission on Service-Learning, 2002) has shown that through academic service learning, students are more likely to become active citizens, "teachers and students tend to become more cohesive as a group" (p. 11), and stakeholders are better able to strengthen community and school connections. I was seeing examples of this almost every time we worked on the project. However, I also was seeing students who were hesitant to take on the responsibility of their own learning. Democratic teaching and critical pedagogy were not ways that these students saw school. However, as the examples I shared show, they were ready to face the challenge brought forth by these practices.

Although in previous years I have always provided choices for my students and opportunities for open discussions, in the end I have decided what we would be learning and when. Academic service learning has been instrumental in the success of introducing democracy in my teaching style. Not only do I feel my students are making connections to the specific academic skills—literacy skills chief among these—that the state requires they learn, but they also are making connections to their own lives and the lives of the people around them, as well as listening and showing respect to their classmates. I could do more to have them become more independent in the process, but much of that is a matter of me giving up some of the power of a *teacher* to become *facilitator*.

These students, far more than any classes I have taught in the past, were more engaged as a group. As I listened to them talk—I really listened— and I heard them agreeing with and complimenting one another, waiting to speak until students finished stating their well-formed thoughts, asking probing questions rather than participating for "a participation grade," and listening to one another and building on one another's ideas. I began to see how our class had formed a working democratic community. As Dewey (1938) stated, "When education is based upon experience and educative experience is seen to be a social process, the situation changes radically. The teacher loses the position of external boss or dictator, but takes on that of leader of group activities" (p. 59). In this case, the students were proving Dewey right.

■ So What? How Our Portraits Reflect Taking Responsibility

Part of what we have tried to show in this chapter is how the directions critical inquiry classrooms take in their learning process frequently seem to hinge on key moments and the ability of teachers and students to recognize those moments as signifiers of shifts in the status quo. Although we suspect all classrooms have similar moments, we argue here that, due to the negotiated nature of critical inquiry, such moments are most likely more plentiful and carry greater import in classrooms where teachers and students inquire with a critical eye. The moments we reported here are not the only pivotal moments that occurred in these classrooms. Some, we suspect, slipped past us unnoticed, despite our attempts to be more attuned to such instances. We elected not to entertain other moments—some of which speak to a range of other issues and some of which resonate with the issues already discussed—due to a lack of time and space.

As we looked across our cases, we noticed some shared characteristics of these moments. To begin, our pivotal moments came during times of uncertainty, particularly instances in which teachers and students renegotiated roles. In Bob's class, Hayley had to see herself as someone who could set the agenda of the class by questioning its purpose, as did Hope's students, Andrea's student Zaria, and the academic service-learning group in Jennifer's class. Rather than yielding to the centripetal pull toward the petrifying of learning roles, students and teachers resisted a singular vision of how learning occurs and of who have and who don't have the expertise to position that learning. Such moments make students and teachers feel unsettled or even threatened because the next steps seem unclear. However, without such moments, students less often take ownership of their learning.

In addition, these cases show the importance of having time to allow processes to take place and experiences to accumulate in order for substantive reflection to occur. Jennifer could have pulled her disappearing act in the third week of school, but we doubt if students would have developed enough shared respect for their work to enable them to pick up the marker she had left behind. Zaria seemed to be a confident learner, but we suspect it was a close relationship that developed over time with Andrea and the shared work of her class that facilitated her willingness not only to be an independent learner but also to be eager to include the class in her quest. Would Hayley have dared to wonder aloud if she were gaining insight in using reading and writing in her mathematics class unless she had sensed through her classroom experience that Bob might have given credence to her question? Likewise, would Hope's students have approached her with their video ideas unless she made it evident to them over time that she, despite their voiced concerns, was not only capable of listening to their ideas, but willing to rethink the agenda with their thoughts in mind?

But the work of learning in critical inquiry classrooms is really more than just providing time and experience. Students must learn content, but, we feel, in ways that are less about recall and more about what Wiggins and McTighe (1998) have called providing for "enduring understanding" (p. 23). Such learning requires that students be able not only to describe a concept, but also to show a deep understanding of that concept by operationalizing, generalizing, and synthesizing the concept. When Bob asked his students to unpack Hayley's question about what they had come to know about content area reading and synthesize the work of the first nine weeks of the course into ways to support struggling readers, he was expecting them to take ownership of their knowledge in ways that reflected their personal understanding of the content. If Bob had only lectured about the importance of connecting reading and writing to content area learning or had provided too early a hard-and-fast definition of how to use literacy in content area classrooms, we seriously doubt if most students in his class could have advanced beyond the mere giving back of what had been told to them. Similarly, when Hope's students created their videos, Jennifer's students developed their school history, and Andrea's student Zaria presented her understanding of the underground railroad, they were demonstrating an enduring understanding of these concepts rather than a definition to be stored in short-term memory and destined to be forgotten. This deep understanding came about because teachers provided time, experience, structure, and support to allow students to explore and internalize these concepts.

What we have described are students and teachers taking greater responsibility for their own learning in formal school situations. From Andrea's second-grade students, through the upper-grades elementary and high school students of Jennifer and Hope, and on to Bob's undergraduates, when given ample opportunity and support to raise their own questions and explore their own issues, students eventually and consistently showed an ability to do so. As previously indicated, time is a factor, and not all students will seize such opportunities equally or with the same confidence. Educators must build experiences that allow for such initiatives on the part of students. And we argue that if more students gain this experience in the lower grades, it will not seem unfamiliar when they are third-year undergraduate students. As teachers, we need to give learners opportunities to grow, not only as decoders and comprehenders but also as meaning makers. Not to provide such opportunity and practice is to assume that students are incapable of such ventures.

Ultimately for our small cohort, it is the recognition of pivotal moments that bears the most significance for teachers and teacher educators. We argue that all classes need a metacognitive component, some way of helping students be more directly aware of what they are learning, how they are learning it, and how that learning might connect to prior and future learning. Educators can't assume, for example, that because students can tell us that their school was once segregated, as in Jennifer's case, that they are able to intuit the significance of such an experience. Nor should we provide them only with our sanctioned interpretations of the significance of such situations. Having provided students with a range of experiences to muck with, explore, and share a range of perspectives on important issues, we need to provide them with opportunities to connect that learning to past learning and to position that learning for future connections.

■ For What? Why Should Teachers and Students Take Responsibility?

The title of this chapter somewhat facetiously alludes to a classic suspense thriller *The Taking of Pelham One Two Three* (Katzka, Scherick, Sargent, & Stone, 1974), a film about the holding of hostages for ransom on a New York subway train. We don't think it pushes our metaphor too far to suggest that too many teachers feel they've been taken hostage in their own classroom and have lost the right to help determine the nature and direction of their pedagogy. Unlike the movie, we who teach don't expect to use the same heavy-handed means to recover what is ours to have. Instead, we seek dialogue that will acknowledge the rights of stakeholders within and out of the classroom and will reflect a range of needs and perspectives.

We are in no way arguing that stakeholders outside the classroom cannot confer standards, expectations, or even assessments upon classrooms. Instead, we return to Shor's (1992) assertion that all stakeholders in education must recognize and constantly negotiate three agendas—that of (1) the student, (2) the teacher, and (3) outside stakeholders. Some equity of representation needs to be achieved. Currently in far too many schools, the petrifying centripetal forces of the outside stakeholders too frequently determine what gets taught, how it gets taught, and what that means for assessment. We who care about education in and for democracy need to reestablish the dialogue among these three agendas in order to tug classrooms away from a stifling and domesticating uniformity. The point is not to swing into a chaos in which all or anything goes but to ensure that schools meet personal and local needs, not just an agenda being voiced at national levels by a vocal minority.

What we have shown in this chapter is that such dialogue can occur without classrooms plunging into anarchy. Rather, what we hope we have made evident is that with some freedom to determine the direction of study comes responsibility. And with that responsibility comes ownership, along with a larger investment in learning. Isn't that what we want of the generations that follow us—an ability to discern, express, explore, and analyze their needs in ways that move in positive directions toward goals that benefit all who participate in our democracy? By creating spaces where students and teachers take greater responsibility for learning, we have created less of a need for outside stakeholders to keep us accountable and control us in ways that can only be seen as belittling and punitive.

Unfortunately, we in our small cohort were too often taking responsibility for the learning in our classrooms in spite of rather than because of the outside agenda. In all cases, we acutely were aware of the many ways, to the point of absurdity, standardized curricula and testing hemmed in our efforts to realize the dialogue we sought. However, such constraints haven't stopped our efforts, as this work shows. Nor did our students suffer from these standards. Rather, given our critical inquiry stances, students became better able to maneuver within formal educational spaces. And dialogue, at least on our part, had begun.

CHAPTER 5

The Risks in Taking on Critical Inquiry Pedagogy

The Stories of Our Questions
The Risk-Taking Cohort

At the time of this study, Bren Daniell was a longtime fifth-grade teacher in the Conyers, Georgia, USA, school district; Jill Hermann-Wilmarth was a novice teacher educator in Athens, Georgia; Michelle Commeyras was a teacher educator at the University of Georgia, Athens; and Sharon Dowling Cox was a veteran speech–language pathologist who, like Bren, worked in Conyers.

Bren Daniell. The issue of being in charge of one's own destiny was something I had managed to overlook when growing up as the only girl in a family of five children in an intensely patriarchal home. Add to that mix a strongly religious background and a rural, working class, southern U.S. environment, and you might not be surprised to find that I had been an adult for a long time before I realized I had the right to an opinion of my own. In addition, I found that I also had the right to disagree. Unfortunately, I was late seeing the light, and for that reason I took it upon myself to give my students a head start, so to speak.

Therefore, when I began considering the question to pursue in my research involving critical inquiry, only one idea immediately surfaced: How can I assist my students in identifying dominant perspectives regarding race, gender, and class in themselves as well as in their peers and the significant adults surrounding them? By recognizing the existence of those perspectives and the manner in which such thinking influenced the way they lived their lives, they would, I hoped, gain power in directing their own.

Sharon Dowling Cox. After completing a specialist degree in reading education, I was enveloped with thoughts about my roles and responsibilities with regard to literacy as a speech–language pathologist. A sense of urgency abounded with the possibilities of using reading to improve language and communication. The critical importance of the interrelationship between a child's language and literacy development and proficiency was paramount to the mastering of the school academic curriculum (Larson & McKinley, 1995; Reed & Spicer, 2003). I was in a unique and exciting position that allowed me to influence both language and literacy skills simultaneously. With this project, I wanted my students and me to use a critical inquiry approach to improve literacy and communication while focusing on academic subjects and curriculum texts.

My initial thoughts focused on critical inquiry pedagogy and questioning in a narrow sense. I imagined how I could engage the students in mediated learning experiences and guide them to become proficient in the use of metacognitive strategies that would increase the significance of student learning. Intervention for language-learning disorders requires the integration of both metacognitive and linguistic strategies if the outcomes of therapy are to enhance the students' effectiveness with language and learning across a variety of academic settings (Singer & Bashir, 1999). When students take ownership of these strategies, they can then use them to guide their efforts and monitor their successes, both in speaking and in learning. I saw critical inquiry pedagogy as a viable way to mediate learning experiences for students to help them understand what they were being taught and why. According to Larson and McKinley (1995), by using mediation to engage students in thinking about their talking, talking about their thinking, and talking about their talking, we can teach them why various communication skills are important. They also note, just as importantly, the need to help students bridge the significance of these skills to other meaningful academic and personal social settings to maximize their potential in using their new communication behaviors in other settings.

My research question became more clearly defined as I shared our class talk about communication with Bren, Jill, and Michelle. When my students demonstrated a weak and very basic understanding and expression of the meaning of the word *communication*, I questioned whether or not we could move forward into stances of critical inquiry pedagogy. I found that the content and manner of my students' responses to this and other questions about communication only yielded a fragment of what they needed to know to be effective communicators. My question was finally born. The perceptive listening of my small cohort helped me to shape my ideas about my practice; students' needs; and knowledge of the connections between literacy, language, and communication to develop my question: How might fifth-grade students with identified language impairments improve their communication skills through critical inquiry?

Jill Hermann-Wilmarth. As a student, I successfully navigated my public school education with the support of my married, heterosexual, white upper middle class parents. Although my teachers did not take risks in their teaching and did not ask me to think outside of the dominant cultural paradigm, my economic and racial privilege ensured that I would not be one of the students who would not be given opportunities to learn about issues not usually discussed in school. My own upbringing is similar to that of most of my undergraduate, preservice elementary education students to whom I teach children's literature and language arts. One of my classroom challenges is to find ways to take risks with my students in ways that encourage them to be teachers who will take risks with and for their students, particularly those students who don't have as many opportunities as their racially and socioeconomically privileged peers might. This challenge led me to ask, What happens when I place a social justice agenda at the center of my teaching? How do students respond both to this agenda and to me as their teacher? And, likewise, how do I respond to my students?

The story of my question is not only my story. A 2003 National School Climate Survey published by the Gay, Lesbian, and Straight Education Network (Kosciw, 2004) reports that 84% of students that they surveyed responded that they have been harassed because of their sexual orientation at school, and 39.1% of these students have been physically assaulted. Other students, such as the children of gay, lesbian, or transgender parents who shared their stories in the 2000 Lambda Literary Award winner for children's literature, *Out of the Ordinary: Essays on Growing up With Gay, Lesbian, and Transgender Parents* (Howey & Samuels, 2000), suffered a similar fear of their differences being discovered and targeted. As an out-lesbian teacher educator who well remembers the sting of "lesbo" and "dyke" being thrown at me as an elementary school student during recesses in the 1980s, and who remembers hearing a fellow teacher in a 2001 graduate multicultural children's literature class say, "Well, if you put garbage in, you get garbage out" about using books with gay or lesbian characters in elementary school, I know that the homophobia of preservice teachers is being ignored, unchallenged, or not presented by teacher educators as a problem in many teacher education programs.

Michelle Commeyras. How can I incorporate critical inquiry pedagogy in university-level courses for undergraduate students learning to teach reading in elementary schools? This has been my research question. It is born of my past and present. In 1986, I completed a Master of Arts degree in critical and creative thinking. As a sixth-grade teacher, I sought to infuse my classroom with opportunities for students to develop themselves as critical and creative thinkers. When I decided to pursue a doctorate, my goal was to specialize in critical thinking within the field of reading education. My dissertation research was an instructional study with a group of fifth-grade students who were identified as "learning disabled." I engaged them in discussions of narrative texts using a lesson format I called "dialogical-thinking reading lessons" (Commeyras, 1993, p. 486).

When I began my new career as a teacher educator, I began wondering about the relationship among terms such as *critical thinking*, *critical literacy*, and *critical inquiry*. I was interested in bringing all these concepts into my teaching in spite of the view that they represented distinct and contravening philosophical assumptions (see Cervetti, Pardales, & Damico, 2001). Also, I was determined to become a more effective educator for those preparing to teach reading in elementary schools. That meant teaching about the National Reading Panel's (National Institute of Child Health and Human Development, 2000) foundations of elementary reading: phonemic awareness, phonics, fluency, vocabulary, and comprehension. My challenge continues to be how to teach from a critical inquiry stance in courses that involve conveying a body of ideas that narrowly construct what counts as text and literacy.

Risk is a word that is charged with potential dangers and rewards on multitudinous levels. Some risks are instantly recognizable, some are subtly cloaked in disguise, and still others are totally obscured from the unsuspecting, inexperienced eye. While risk is inherent in all facets of life, my concern is how it relates to my professional life as a teacher and how that also impacts my personal life. (Bren Daniell)

During the two years we met as a cohort and with the larger community of teacher researchers, we talked about feelings of risk. Much of what has been written about the concept of risk pertains to financial investment, insurance, health and safety, and the environment. Risk analysis or risk assessment concerns itself with reducing undesirable effects through appropriate modification of the causes or mitigation of the consequences (Renn, 1992). Risk, in this sense, has not been of much concern in education. According to historians Tyack and Cuban (1995), education through public schooling has remained remarkably stable over the years, and they conclude that there has been "a good deal of continuity in how teachers taught" (p. 86). Granted, there have been reforms and innovations, but they "become assimilated to previous patterns of schooling" (p. 83). Change is difficult given that the basic "grammar of schooling" (p. 85) has remained stable over the decades. The "deep grammar of schooling" (Lankshear & Knobel, 2003, p. 30) does *not* stress critical inquiry pedagogy, social justice, and students becoming self-directed with regard to their own learning. This is particularly true in the current educational climate in which federal legislation is based on a conservative ideology that emphasizes scripted literacy instruction and the idea that teaching literacy skills and strategies can be a neutral process (Edmondson, 2004).

Father Luigi Giussani, who teaches theology, writes in *The Risk of Education* (2001) that we must insist on an education that is critical. He means *critical* in the sense of the Greek words *krinen* and *krisis*. He does not mean critical in a negative sense. To Giussani, being critical is an "invitation to try to understand what one is faced with, to discover a new good, a new truth, to extract a more mature and deeper sense of satisfaction" (p. 10). The purpose Giussani has in mind is to "free the young from mental slavery and from the tendency to conform, which mentally enslaves them to the forces in society" (p. 11). Giussani tells his students on the first day of class:

I'm not here so that you can take my ideas as your own; I'm here to teach you a true method that you can use to judge the things I will tell you. And what I

have to tell you is the result of a long experience, of a past that is two thousand years old. (p. 11)

While fulfilling the educational goal of teaching about the past and its traditions, we also agree with Giussani that education must be critical.
Education that is critical, in Giussani's terms, can be risky because we are
teaching ways of thinking that might lead students to question or doubt received knowledge from their family, religion, and government.

All risk concepts deal with possibilities. Risk is about the possibility that
something undesirable may occur as a result of natural events or human
activities. However, risk also is about the possibility that a desirable outcome
may become a reality. Thus, as we pursued critical inquiry pedagogy as literacy educators, we implicitly addressed the following questions:

1. What uncertainties would concern us?

2. What undesirable outcomes did we fear?

3. What desirable outcomes did we seek?

■ Portraits of Risk in Critical Inquiry Pedagogy

Bren's Classroom:
Investigating Our Social and Cultural Perspectives

When embarking on the use of critical inquiry, I had not expected close
personal scrutiny of myself by students or me. After watching the movie
Ruby Bridges (Palcy, 1998), the well-known story of an African American
girl who integrated an all–European American school in the 1950s, I was
stopped dead in my tracks by an inquisitive, thoughtful student, Tyrone,
when he asked, "Ms. Daniell, would you have been like the whites in the
movie if you had been around during the beginning of integration?"

I gave careful, but rapid thought as my students sat, silent and attentive. My mind flashed back to the fear that engulfed me during my first year
of teaching—the fear of being transferred to an all–African American
school with no time to prepare for such a totally new situation in midyear.
I wanted my response to be truthful, and I didn't want the students to think
ill of me. Sometimes those two desires seemed incompatible. What I told
Tyrone was that I didn't think that I would have acted in that hateful way
and that I hoped I wouldn't have, but that when everyone around you is

acting a certain way (meaning the majority of the southern U.S. European American culture at that time), it is not easy to say what one would do. Although he had no further comment, I felt he understood my dilemma; we previously had discussed a similar situation in *Shiloh* (Naylor, 2000), in which the young boy Marty wanted to act to save the dog, but his dad make it clear that people at that time did not give a lot of consideration to the welfare of animals. My students' opinions of me, which I valued, and my opinion of myself were at risk. It was a sickening feeling.

When I began my critical inquiry research project, I struggled to formulate an appropriate question for the ability level of fifth-grade students that would lead them to inquire about social issues. During a course on sociopolitical perspectives taught by Michelle Commeyras, it had become glaringly apparent to me that many teachers and students are often unaware of the social agendas and the power situations at work in a typical classroom. Three distinct and distant memories from my early public schooling surfaced as we, the students in Michelle's class, delved into the politics inherent in all classrooms.

My first memory involved a tall, skinny girl who sat on the left side of our fifth-grade classroom. Her long, scraggly blond hair; deadpan, lifeless face; and seemingly unclean appearance came clearly to mind. I still remember her name after 40-plus years. The feeling that accompanied that image was a sad one, mixed with my own curiosity of what happened to her after our school began to group students according to their academic ability. Although I can't remember seeing her past the fifth grade, I've often wondered what happened to that unengaged, stone-faced person once she was shuttled off to a group of similarly uninvolved students. While sensing that something was not quite right, I was, at age 11, unaware of the dangers and injustices that sometimes occur in such ability groupings.

The second repugnant memory, before school desegregation occurred, centered around a letter being read to my seventh-grade class by one of my teachers, whose image and name remain fresh in my mind. As an adult today, I resent her manner and intent in reading that letter, but as a child I was oblivious to the politics in her actions. I'm sorry to say I can't remember the content, but I do acutely remember the purpose for reading it—humiliating and shaming the writer and others of his culture. The letter, with all its grammatical errors and failures to communicate, had been written as an entry for a county competition by a seventh-grade student from an African American school, and the teacher read it to us to demonstrate their inferiority and to validate separation of the races. What untold damage in conceptions was accomplished that day!

The third example in which teachers wielded politics in the classroom occurred during my entire senior year of high school. My U.S. history teacher and the senior class's sponsor, a dyed-in-the-wool southern U.S. rebel, used her position to influence her students' thinking. Under her direction, senior superlative pictures were taken of students dressed in replicas of Confederate uniforms and antebellum dresses. The site of our senior prom was enshrined in the *Gone with the Wind* (Selznick, Howard, & Fleming, 1939) motif, and our yearbook's copy lamented the glorious days of yore with sappy sentimentality and wispy clouds. In addition, she inundated class lectures with negative comments about Yankees. Often, I have jokingly commented that I was well out of high school before I realized that the South had actually lost the American Civil War.

These memories contributed heavily to my decision to include dialogue in my classroom around social issues found in carefully selected chapter books. I hoped to help my students better understand themselves and others within the context of their cultures, possibly to redefine some of the concepts society has handed down, and ultimately to give them more power over their own lives. Of particular concern were the many years it had taken me to discover and to halfway comprehend how my ideas and opinions were shaped as the result of the power issues played out by the adults charged with my education. Somewhat resentful at having not been more in the driver's seat of my own life, I determined to give my students the jumpstart I had missed.

James Baldwin (1988) stated it more eloquently:

> As one begins to become conscious one begins to examine the society in which he is being educated. The purpose of education, finally, is to create in a person the ability to look at the world for himself, to make his own decisions, to say to himself, this black or this is white, to decide for himself whether there is a God in heaven or not. To ask questions of the universe, and then to learn to live with those questions, is the way he achieves his own identity. (p. 4)

As a result, my critical inquiry efforts targeted the development of consciousness by assisting the students in identifying their own perspectives on social issues as well as the differing perspectives of classmates, authors, and society in general. I felt uncertain about how to proceed because of the mix of races, genders, and religions in a typical classroom. Most of my inquiry efforts occurred within my language arts group that was composed of 11 remedial students. Although the composition varied due to new arrivals from other school systems and classes within our school, typically the membership included two African American males and five European American females ranging in ages from 10 to 11. The membership and the small size of the group were determined by the students' remedial performance on the culminating achievement tests in fourth grade.

What risks did I intentionally take? First, I abandoned the system-provided and recommended basal reading series, something I had never done before. I felt this was a risk because the school system administrators had trained me to use the stories, procedures, and questions supplied within the basal lessons, and I had not previously provided opportunities for students to create their own questions or to veer away from the provided "correct" responses. After abandoning the basal reading series, I devoted considerable time to becoming acquainted with many children's books, mostly by listening to them on tape. As a result, I became enthralled with audio books and saw no reason that the children would not do the same. Based on years of teaching, I was confident that students would benefit in fluency, vocabulary, and enjoyment from listening and reading with the professionals who record audio books. However, I did not know if that would translate into higher language arts test scores. Because one of my goals was to assist in creating lifelong readers, not just good test takers, I thought the risk worth taking.

Second, I chose chapter books whose content provided opportunities to discuss social issues: *Shiloh* (Naylor, 2000), *Chocolate Fever* (Smith, 1972/1989), *The Friendship* (Taylor, 1998), *Roll of Thunder, Hear My Cry* (Taylor, 1976), *Our Only May Amelia* (Holm, 2001), and *Kapitau and the Magic Whistle* (Mushonga, 2001; an African folk tale). For our critical inquiry dialogues about the selections, I asked the students to generate their own questions. This approach differed from my prior practice of asking detail and inference questions with predetermined "right" answers. I devoted a disproportionate amount of time for discussion and less time for isolated skill lessons while fearing the effect on spring standardized and criterion test scores. I had no way of knowing how extended in-depth discussion would translate into scores on the Stanford Achievement Test (the ninth edition) and a state-mandated criterion test. These uncertainties caused me endless concern and worry.

As fate would have it, the Stanford Achievement Test scores for the year were found by state system administrators to be invalid due to huge scoring errors. However, I did find validation in the results of the state-mandated criterion-referenced test; all my remedial students passed. Unfortunately, no tests exist to document the motivation, engagement, enjoyment, and degree of empathy I observed in my students from being allowed to openly discuss questions and to identify and clarify their perspectives.

Our first book, *Shiloh*, was rich in opportunities to discuss issues such as lying, stealing, developing relationships with parents and other adults, abusing animals, and committing oneself to action to correct a wrongdoing. The students became deeply engaged in discussing whether or not Marty, the main character, was justified in hiding another character's abused dog and lying to prevent the return of the dog to an abusive situation. Students expressed their own feelings and disagreed with one another while we practiced nonjudgmentally listening and respecting opposing views. Because there was no sanctioned right or wrong answer, each student thoughtfully worked toward his or her individual conclusion. This took time, and I constantly repressed the fear of spending too much time talking and listening instead of proceeding quickly and perfunctorily through a list of skills.

Chocolate Fever, our second selection, at first seemed light on social issues, but unexpectedly led to a discussion of stereotypes, a concern we would return to many times during discussions of other books. During one book-related activity, I noted that none of the students listed the race of an influential character in the story. From early conversations surrounding this book emerged the information that the students thought it impolite to discuss race and skin color. Indeed, Shaun, one of the two African Americans in the group, said he would refuse to participate in any such discussions.

Using critical inquiry created another uncertainty. While I recognized the value in allowing students to generate their own questions to discuss openly, honestly, and without fear of disapproval, I also recognized the risks. Could we trust one another enough to express our thoughts and not penalize one another for thinking perhaps differently than others? When disagreeing, would tempers flare? Could we negotiate the issues without offending one another? In taking up the social issues agenda, I agonized over whether I would be able to deal with the use of racially offensive language in *The Friendship* and *Roll of Thunder, Hear My Cry*. Now I can say yes to all of those questions, but at the onset I did not know.

The most risk-charged decision I made during the year was in choosing to read *The Friendship*, which not only used the word *nigger* but also targeted some widely held views about African American–European American race relations. After prereading the book, I was not sure it was appropriate. Not only did the book contain racial slurs, but it also concluded with an event in which a European American man, John, shoots an old African American man, Tom. How would my African American students feel? How would my non–African American students feel? I had no idea, so I loaned the book to my friend and soon-to-be cohort member Sharon Dowling Cox to get her opinion as a teacher and as an African American. After discussing my dilemma with her, she said, "Do it! The students seldom, if ever, have the opportunity to discuss such issues."

Having worked with our new principal for only a few months, I was uncertain of his reaction if parents became upset over the racial slurs and violent content. Therefore, I sought his counsel. First, he asked me if *The Friendship* was shelved in our school library. It was. Then after reading the book and agreeing that the content was intense, he offered me his support with any of the lessons if I needed it.

I sent a brief synopsis of the book home in a letter to parents, explaining that the word *nigger* was used in the book and offering them the opportunity to read it. Only one parent requested to preview the book, and no parents forbade participation.

During the several days it took to read and to discuss the book, I was thrilled to find that the students did not appear to harbor ill will toward people of other races. They related experiences from their own lives that let the members of the group know their perspectives about what they considered fair treatment of people. In fact, they identified compassionately with Tom, the old man shot by John. They wrote songs, prose, and poems sympathetic to Tom while railing against the offensive unfair treatment he received from John.

I also had concerns for Shaun, who had previously stated that he would not discuss racial issues. Would he refuse to participate? Would he act out on his discomfort? Neither happened.

Initially, Shaun appeared nervous and wiggly and avoided looking at me or anyone else when we talked in a small-group setting. However, as we waded along in potentially treacherous waters, Shaun appeared more comfortable and finally settled down with the process. In fact, he responded with comments when asked by me, other students, or both and even occasionally volunteered his thoughts. Tyrone, the other African American student within the group, quite openly asked questions, stated his opinions, and related events in the story to events in his own personal life. This young student would be the one who consistently throughout the year asked troubling, pointed, thoughtful questions and made astute comments and connections that I attributed to our use of critical inquiry.

Similarly, during her speech–language sessions, Sharon also was taking risks with students.

Sharon's Classroom: Inviting Complexity and Elaboration in "Talking Detours"

Like Bren, I wanted to create a different kind of talk with my students. I explored critical inquiry pedagogy with a group of three students—Malik, John, and Jada—who had identified language impairments. To illustrate what I learned with these students, I will focus on Malik. He was a fifth-grade African American who had been receiving services to address language impairment for approximately two and a half years. He was a very polite, cheerful young boy, who, after experiencing years of academic difficulties, seemed to take the almost daily questions about missing homework assignments in stride. When Malik began therapy, he had severe semantic deficits that compromised his ability to comprehend and express himself orally and in writing.

My goals for Malik were to improve his receptive and expressive language development. Specifically, he began therapy with a three-year delay in expressive vocabulary. He had difficulty being aware of categories and relations in all aspects of language, which compromised his ability to understand and formulate ideas and concepts represented in his curriculum texts. His oral sentence complexity was simplistic, and, as a result, he misunderstood advanced syntactical forms and did not consistently or efficiently process information that he read. In addition, he lacked an awareness of communication breakdowns and a limited repertoire of repair strategies.

With the recent completion of a professional degree in reading education, I had wholeheartedly embraced my responsibility as a speech–language pathologist (SLP) to address literacy issues within the domains of communication disorders (American Speech-Language-Hearing Association, 2001). Infusing reading education methods into therapy sessions by focusing on phonological awareness, metacognitive strategies, and the use of graphic organizers to improve vocabulary and comprehension was a familiar component to my language therapy sessions since completing my degree in reading education. However, to introduce critical inquiry pedagogy to areas (language and academics) in which students such as Malik already struggled seemed risky and problematic. For me, critical inquiry required analytical thought processes and cohesive communication skills that were very advanced for my students with language disorders. Therefore, I anticipated that taking this risk would require me to increase expectations and accelerate my students; however, I did not foresee that it would require me to change my instructional ways of talking.

There are probably as many treatment approaches to address speech and language disorders as there are such disorders. To improve oral communication, traditional intervention procedures have systematically taught phonology (articulation), syntax (grammar), semantics (concepts), and pragmatics (social communication, functional language) as isolated skill areas (Larson & McKinley, 1995). Many intervention approaches use behaviorally based methodology designed to elicit or expand communication through teacher-led, structured situations. An SLP targets areas of a student's weakness to provide concentrated opportunities, along with scaffolding and reinforcement, to increase the student's awareness and purposeful use of the targeted structures. Because there is no set curriculum, many SLPs use decontextualized material (i.e., materials that target specific but narrow objectives and have little direct connection to the curriculum in the students' content area classrooms or their lives as a whole). One of the challenges inherent in pull-out programs in which content is separate from curricular areas is that students find it difficult to connect learning in the speech and language classroom with learning in the regular education classroom. The positive side of this autonomy is the SLP's freedom to more effectively coordinate the intervention approach and thus to maximize the students' overall language and communication skills. What I found was that using an inquiry-based approach, instead of a more structured therapy discourse, allowed us to link reading and writing from content area classes with extensive opportunities to use oral language in meaningful communicative interactions.

On the first day of our inquiry, I asked the students to write about four questions:

1. What is communication?
2. Why is communication important?

3. What makes communication clear?

4. What do I do to make my communication clear?

I asked the students to listen to one another's responses and rate their peers' communication as "clear" or "unclear."

"Comm-comm-communi-communication..." Malik began haltingly as he responded to the first question. Malik's noticeable difficulty in articulating this word struck me as odd because he typically did not struggle with word formulation. His struggle was characteristic of a person attempting to say an unfamiliar word for the first time. But how could this be? Malik continued, "Communication is when you talk to somebody and however you communicate." John and Jada rated Malik's response as "clear."

I was perplexed. The phrase "however you communicate" seemed ambiguous and thus problematic. So I probed, "You thought his message was clear? What did he say?"

John replied, "I forgot." This sent us on a detour. We needed to address attentive listening.

I asked, "If you forgot, what can you do?"

"Make him read it again," John said.

Now, I thought, get ready for a pragmatic language detour.

"Make him read it again?" I repeated, emphasizing the word *make*. "You could ask him to read it over again."

"Read it over again," John commanded. This command was apparently acceptable to Malik, which was typical of his easygoing nature.

Cheerfully, Malik repeated, "Communication is when you talk to somebody and however you communicate."

"OK, what did he say?" I inquired wanting to hear them put in their own words their understanding of Malik's message.

"Communication is when you talk to somebody," John replied.

John had simplified Malik's message but kept it semantically and syntactically intact. I felt a release of tension at having my expectations confirmed that having John restate Malik's message was within his ability level.

It was in reflecting on this first session that I came to the idea that an inquiry approach necessitated *talking detours*, those unpredictable changes in the directions of our conversations that occurred when I asked the students to be accountable for their learning in new ways. I became increasingly aware that these detours were necessary in preparing my students to be aware of the complexities of language communication. I, too, was on a detour from traditional therapy dialogue.

I often used intervention strategies that relied on structured discourse such as Request-Response-Evaluation (RRE). This is a common structure in many therapies as well as classroom settings (Leahy, 2004). The SLP initiates the conversation, the student responds, and the SLP comments, often evaluating the student's communicative competence. The orderliness and adherence to participant roles in this type of structured therapeutic discourse positions the SLP as the authority figure and the student as the subordinate figure (Leahy, 2004). It can be used effectively to teach discrete skills; however, it provides fewer opportunities for student control and responses. In promoting critical inquiry pedagogy with my students, I found that I moved away from an RRE structure toward a more dialogic format that invited complexity and elaboration.

I began asking Malik and his two peers to share what they were learning in their school subjects by summarizing, comparing, or stating opinions and ideas. This approach removed the pressure on them to know the "right" answers while still allowing me to assess their ability to communicate content knowledge through dialogue rather than the RRE format. The following is an example from our first dialogue on the U.S. Civil War.

Sharon: What, if anything, surprised you in your reading?

John: There were many people that died.

Sharon: There were many people that died. Did any numbers jump out at you?

Malik: Um, what the weirdest thing that was about me [what surprised me] that the northern side had many troops and the, uh, Confederates had lesser. But I wonder, how did the northern side win 'cause 360,000 troops died on the northern side and 260,000, um, troops died on the um, the uh, Confederacy side?

Sharon: Did we understand Malik's question? What did he say?

Jada: He said that he was surprised about how many, uh, people died in the North because of how they can win because they lost a lot of people and the South lost less.

At first, it was difficult for me to ignore errors in grammar and syntax, articulation, or prosody, and instead to keep my focus primarily on the content of the students' messages. Were they comprehending information and could they express their knowledge and learning with others? To encourage the students to communicate freely, I avoided taking an evaluative stance as a therapist until we replayed our tape recorded conversations and analyzed our performances through objective ratings and feedback at that time. If and when students had difficulty, discussion around the recordings was my opportunity to be explicit and to guide them to use strategies to improve their understanding of the subject material and to effectively communicate their learning.

As a means of self-reflection and -evaluation, the students wrote in a journal about their content learning and self-evaluated their communication skills using a rubric with scores 1–5. The rubric I had designed for clear communication called for attention to (a) word usage, (b) appropriate vocabulary, (c) sentence complexity, and (d) correct information. To achieve clearer communication, I encouraged the students to (a) restate ideas, (b) use different words, (c) modify sentence structure, (d) adjust their rate of speech, (e) alter their volume level, and (f) use sources to support or confirm the accuracy of their information. Using that rubric, the students were asked to rate their in-class and group participation with the following scale:

1. (0–1): I contributed very little to the class discussion.
2. (2–3): I gave some contribution to the class discussion. I did not add any of my own thoughts.
3. (4–5): I shared thinking about subjects in new ways. I talked about my ideas with the group. I used reading material to support my talk.

At first, Malik had difficulty understanding how to rate his communication efforts, and he did little more than copy the ratings description in his written evaluation. The resulting contradiction can be seen in his response of December 3, 2002, in which he wrote the following:

> Today I Learned how the civil war ended and started. I Learned that the northern side won the civil war and because they had more factories and more supplies and Land. and I also Learned that more people died in the north than In the south and that's what I Learned. My communication. I contributed very little to class discussion 3 some contribution to the discussion, shared thinking about subject in new ways.

It's fairly evident in the excerpt above that Malik is just copying indiscriminately from the rubric, without much thought being put into his self-assessment. However, as Malik grew more comfortable with the rubric, his self-assessment became more complex. On December 17, 2002, Malik wrote:

today I Learned that the North had more factories and more steel and iron in the factories, but the south only had slaves and I also Learned in the south before the war the south was more ready, because the already ready, because They was tread [trained] to shoot Guns and riding hourses and fishing and that why they was more ready for the war. today I will give My self a 4 four because I did priticapate in class and sometimes I picked up stuff that I dint soppos to and I was loud and understandable, that why I Gave myuself a four"

Although mechanically there is much to be desired here, in this excerpt Malik shows a much richer sense of his own performance in my class. He not only knows what he came to understand but also has a solid sense of how he participated.

My students and I also inquired into socially appropriate ways to ask for clarification from those they did not understand. On January 16, 2002, Malik offered Jada advice during a small-group session regarding her communication, and his response reflected a growing understanding of his ability to use the rubric to give useful and accurate feedback to his peers:

She should have said, the north had more factories and railroads. And it wasn't clear. One reason, didn't speak loud enough and some part was true information and some were not.

At our last session, I asked Malik and his peers to discuss what they had learned about communication. Malik replied,

I learned that if, like, if you come up to a person and you talk and he don't know what you said, the person ask you to repeat it. You will have to say it clearly and use different speech and use correct information, and he or she or somebody will probably understand what you said.

With some students, pursuing the dual goals of improving communication while encouraging critical inquiry pedagogy can offer SLPs a unique perspective on student learning and provide a direct link to schoolwide curriculum and objectives. During many class sessions I was cautiously aware that I could not fully predict the direction our dialogue might take us. I learned to adapt to the students' needs as I strived to help them understand their own strengths and difficulties and to accept responsibility for improving their communication and learning skills; I felt humbled. I began to see Malik build intrinsic motivation as he experienced increased confidence and competence in areas of communication. Granted, our talking detours sometimes felt as risky as traveling through California's Big Sur on the beautiful but treacherous 89-mile highway winding down the coast of California to its breathtaking valleys, never expecting what is just around every sharp turn. You want to extend time as you attempt to maneuver the moment—to hold your breath as you behold new and rugged terrain. At other times, our detours were as delightful as traveling on a free-flowing highway—direct and quick. Promoting critical inquiry pedagogy in the pursuit of communicative competence can enable students to better produce and assess their intellectual skills and also can lead them to becoming more reflective readers, writers, listeners, and speakers.

Jill's Classroom: Self-Interrogating Our Stances to Focus on Social Justice

I have been grappling with what it means to teach from an ethical and honest position. After realizing that requiring my students to share in class their writing about their lives also required me to share my life with them (hooks, 1994), I began taking a different stance in my classroom. In my second year of teaching university students to be elementary school teachers, I focused on the risks that I could take with my students and reflected on my actions in the hope of employing Freire's (1970/1993) definition of *praxis*: "reflection and action upon the world in order to transform it" (p. 33).

In my efforts to teach in an honest manner, I have become an increasingly out-lesbian teacher (i.e., I do not try to hide my sexual orientation, and when I am in conversation with others, I speak about my family and partner in much the same way that my heterosexual colleagues and students speak about their families). Although outing myself is risky, particularly while teaching in the conservative climate of a southern U.S. university, I feel that I can become for my students "another kind of text" (Mittler & Blumenthal, 1994, p. 4), helping them to put a face to the importance of multiculturally reading and thinking. As I grapple with the complexities of creating rapport with my students from outside the closet door, I have become more deeply committed to teaching from a critical inquiry stance with an intentional focus on social justice.

Although I am certainly tied to my own experiences of marginalization, this commitment also comes from seeing how easily teachers and professors choose to ignore issues of oppression in their classrooms. Too little time, the lack of a visible minority, uneasiness, and ignorance all contribute to the silencing of the histories and realities of those who are marginalized. My seat both at the table and in the margins gives me a sense of urgency around the ways that issues of social justice are or are not a part of school culture.

Because I am committed to this social justice stance, I required myself to not only teach from outside the closet door but also to ask my students to think about and discuss issues that might make us uncomfortable. I think of Bob Fecho's (2004) discussion of *threat* in critical inquiry classrooms, and quite noticeably threat is there and is critical to the inquiry I do in my teaching. I never know how my students will react. This critical stance, along with and in addition to readings and assignments with radical agendas, certainly disrupted the image of what my students thought children's literature or a language arts methods class could look and feel like. It forced them to see that teachers do not always reproduce the status quo culture that is often presented as fact or as the only way to teach.

It also has made me feel as if I was hitting a brick wall again and again and again. In the first year of this study, students resisted conversations about class and sexual orientation. Even the few students who read and enjoyed books with gay or lesbian characters, such as *Holly's Secret* (Garden, 2000), or enthusiastically discussed and agreed with articles that address the problem of censorship of these books, such as *Reading, Writing, and Censorship: When Reading Good Books Can Get Schools in Trouble* (Miner, 1998), did not see how bringing these books into their classrooms was either appropriate or their responsibility. Students met attempts to challenge gender norms with rolling their eyes, and discussions about race typically, but not always, began and ended with, "I'm not racist, but...." My course evaluations affirmed for me that my approach had fallen short— students' comments, such as "This is not a multicultural education class, so we should just stick to writing methods," abounded.

Where had I gone wrong? I had been honest and reflective about my own actions. I had been open and risky as hooks (1994) required. I brought my frustrations to one of our critical inquiry pedagogy large-cohort meetings. Bob said that my students needed to take an interrogative stance of themselves for new ground to be broken and for growth to really happen around the issues of gender and sexuality. As I evaluated and inquired into my teaching practices, I realized that I wasn't providing the students with the spaces for this interrogation to occur. I believe that text is anything that we can make meaning of, and it seems that the text of our classroom was not, as I had hoped, about the language, discourse, and experiences of marginalized people but about layers of defensiveness. We too often were in an ideological debate.

While reading essays in the anthology *Tilting the Tower: Lesbians, Teaching, Queer Subjects* (Garber, 1994), I was reminded again why I had begun to require myself to use particular language in my classroom and to raise challenging issues. Adams and Emery (1994) write, "when we allow the energy of our authentic selves, hard fought for and deep in us, to inform our teaching, our students rise to the challenge" (p. 31). So, on the first day of another semester of my children's literature class, I asked students to think about the stances from which they read. After a few blank stares, I gave the example that I am a feminist and that I cannot take that ideological stance away from anything that I read. I asked them to think about race, class, gender, religion, sexuality, and regionality and gave them about 10 minutes and a piece of construction paper on which to write.

I was a little disappointed in the sharing that came after the activity—some wrote their race on the page, but only "because you said to." How, besides actually reading literature by and about people who are different than my students, would I help them to think about and explore ideas of privilege and marginalization? I was out as a lesbian in class, and I required my students to read Delpit (1995) and others who challenge privileged cultural norms in their classrooms. Somehow, however, classroom talk around these issues never surfaced in meaningful ways—in small groups, the voices of a few determined the paths of conversation. It seemed that my questions about race or language or difference were discussed when I entered the conversation but forgotten when I moved on to the next group.

I learned, from my course evaluations, by the end of the first year of the study that my students did not see my teaching stance as risky but rather as an imposition. The course evaluations showed that they felt that *only* my voice counted and that my "liberal agenda" was too forced. My students were aware of the power that I held as the teacher and saw that as the only power working in the classroom. I was tempted to disregard the sometimes untrue ("The articles we read had to do with how white people are evil and racist, rich people suck, and that homosexuality should be taught in the classroom") and sometimes cruel words that my students wrote in their anonymous course evaluations; however, my semester-long disengagement with student need or voice—my ignoring of student resistance to the topics raised in class—seemed to have ended any possibility of students seeing the power of their own social positions. I had to take another risk, and this time it was listening to the resistance of my students and learning how to negotiate that resistance with future students.

Delpit (1995) wrote, "Those with power are frequently least aware of—or least willing to acknowledge—its existence. Those with less power are often most aware of its existence" (p. 24). Some of my students were able to point out easily the power that my position as teacher provided me within our classroom, but, in turn, felt entitled to the power and privilege provided by their own race, class, and expressed sexual orientation. Reading about and talking about how being European American is a privilege had never occurred to many of my students before, and the concept seemed an argument, rather than an idea, to many of them. Without any awareness of the power that race, socioeconomic status, or heterosexuality carries, self-interrogation of privilege would prove a challenge. In Shor's (1992) approach to emancipatory and liberatory education, reflexive teaching "implies orienting subject matter to student culture—their interests, needs, speech, and perceptions—while creating a negotiable openness in class where the students' input jointly creates the learning process" (p. 16). I had to find a space to enter into dialogue with my students that wouldn't lead to their silent resistance. I decided to use the chapter "Reading Multiculturally" by Hade (1997) to lead my next group of students into critical inquiry pedagogy.

Hade uses the movie *The Lion King* (McArthur, Schumaker, Allers, & Minkoff, 2003) to begin his discussion of how to read multiculturally, pointing to the overt sexism and racism in the movie. He goes on to write about the importance of teachers reading about issues of race, class, and gender in children's literature and then talking about these issues with students. He notes that "reading is inherently social and is dominated by culture. And the meanings we hold about race, class, and gender, many of which may be stereotypes, mediate how we interpret text" (p. 235). He also writes that "silence is the oxygen of racism and bigotry" (p. 237). His essay implores teachers to teach their students how to read for signs of racism, classism, and sexism in order to dispel stereotypes of marginalized groups. How would my students react?

My students were required to respond by e-mail to the texts that we read before each class. After reading Hade's chapter, the e-mails began pouring in. The responses were more varied than I could have imagined—it seemed that some students had been so offended by Hade's negative reaction to *The Lion King* that they had stopped reading the article altogether. Others wrote of how this article helped them rethink their past experiences of reading "white" books with nonwhite students. Most students took the time to articulate their opinions—in agreement or disagreement with the text—with citations from the article and well-formed arguments or examples.

Then, the language of one student caused a physical reaction—I had to look away from the computer screen. "This is the most retarded thing I've ever read," she wrote. There was no well-articulated argument about why she disagreed with Hade's position. It seemed that she had not only missed the entire purpose of the article but also had not thought about her stance as a future teacher. I wondered how many other students used language this way and what would happen if they did so in an elementary school classroom. I thought about all of my other questions that I asked my students about written and oral voice and the discipline of our classroom. How could I bring to the class all of the varied voices of my students in ways that felt and looked different—that took us out of the comfort that small groups of four or five offered, but didn't expose us to silence? How could I value the voices of my students and challenge them at the same time? How could I continue discussion of these issues without that discussion being viewed as my own agenda?

The next time students walked into class, there were no tables or desks to sit in, just a huge circle of chairs. The directions on the board read, "Bring only your text with you to a chair. Leave everything else along the walls of the room." As we sat together, in the very open circle, students reported later feeling quite exposed—vulnerable without the tables to protect them. We had 10 minutes to find quotes from the reading that were meaningful because they angered or resonated with them. Then, beginning at a random place in the circle, and with no explanation, we read aloud our quotes. Some of us read more than one time, and we often repeated text.

After listening to one another read the words we had already read silently and written on paper, I passed out strips of paper. Using quotes from student e-mail responses, I created a script that addressed the main issues and feelings that Hade's article invoked. On each strip of paper was a sentence from that script. Each student was given a sentence, and we went from student to student, each reading a script. When we finished, there was a long silence. Students in the past had informed me that my voice was the only one that counted in our classroom. Now, we were thinking with one another in a different format than we were used to. We were seeing one another's and our own words in new ways.

I interrupted our silence by asking them to form small, safe groups to talk about the experience. I acknowledged the power that I had had in choosing which statements and sentiments were included and asked students to talk about that. I also asked them to talk about what it felt like to hear their own words come out of other people's mouths, if they would have written differently had they known I would use their ideas in such a way, the effectiveness of reading Hade's words aloud before reading their own, and any other issues that the activity brought up for them. When I joined the groups, I asked if they better understood the concept of ideological stance and of reading multiculturally. Students seemed excited—some said that they would be responding to the assigned children's literature differently, some wanted to reread Hade's article, some said that they wanted to edit their e-mails before sending them. I also asked them to e-mail me by the end of the week about the process and the class—to let me know if the format worked for them.

I was surprised by the responses that students wrote over and over in their "reaction to the class": "I now know that you actually read what we write." "It felt good to know that you care about what I say." "I want my students to know that I listen to them, too." In reflecting on how my theory was and was not feeding my practice—in rethinking, reviewing, interrogating, and using my theory differently—I am able to see my students and the possibilities in our classroom in new ways. In the same event of teaching and learning about reading literature in new ways, my students and I learned how we can teach and learn from one another in ways that value multiple perspectives, give voice to different ways of thinking, and help us to look at and listen to our own words multiple times.

How we, as teachers, experience risk in our classrooms varies by experience, student, and context. Michelle's students often come to class desiring a formula for how to teach reading. She interrupted student expectations surrounding what reading can look, sound, or feel like, but she wondered, was that a risk?

Michelle's Classroom: Wanting Preservice Teachers to Examine Their Assumptions About Language

I realized a connection between my young activist self and my much older university professor self when analyzing my decision to show the scene "Amethyst Rocks" from the movie *Slam* (Levin, Stratton, Williams, Sohn, &

Kessler, 1998) in my reading education course that comprised 24 students preparing to be elementary school teachers. *Slam* begins with the protagonist, Raymond Joshua, played by real-life poet Saul Williams, walking away from the Capitol building in Washington, DC, USA. Soon thereafter, the police arrest him for selling a small amount of marijuana. It is clearly a shock for him as a small-time dealer and street poet when he enters the violent world of prison life. The scene I showed takes place in the prison yard when Raymond is about to be confronted by two rival gangs. His fellow inmates want to know where his allegiance lies. Raymond deals with this pressure with fiery, impassioned words—in poetic form. The gang members listen and are speechless. They are thinking about his message while Raymond walks away without committing to either gang.

In 1973, as a 20-year-old, I joined the Peaceful Movement Committee, a prison reform group that met at the Massachusetts State Correctional Institution in Concord, Massachusetts, USA, where I lived and had attended K–12 public schools. I attended weekly meetings with incarcerated men and their family and friends. I recall how impressed and surprised I was by the eloquence of these men in prison. Most were African American, and I was French American. They were smart, friendly, and wise. It was then I realized that I had learned the stereotype that people in prison were not as intelligent as those who were law abiding. When I showed the film clip of Raymond reciting "Amethyst Rocks," I was not thinking about how my past contributed to my decision to use this with students. I had found the story of Raymond, the poet in and out of prison, compelling. I wanted to show something from it to my European American female students whom I suspected had not yet had much contact with urban African Americans. I wanted them to see how Raymond used his poetic sensibilities to defend himself and to raise the consciousness of his prison brothers. Far from my consciousness at the time was my great-grandmother Jessie Donaldson Hodder (born March 30, 1867). She developed the prison reforms that became the model for the United States by giving female prisoners dignity, a chance to reform, and the opportunity for an education. Now, in retrospect, it makes sense that my personal biography played a role in taking the risk to show this scene that I feared would offend my students because it included profanities.

So what was risky in showing an excerpt from the movie *Slam* in which Raymond delivers his poem "Amethyst Rocks" in a prison setting? In retrospect, the risks seemed low, but nonetheless, at the time I hesitated—I wondered—I showed the video segment at the very end of a class, leaving no time for discussion. It felt risky because I was trying to create rapport with a new cohort of students who would be with me for two semesters. Based on more then 10 years of teaching other preservice teachers, I knew that my success depended largely on what kind of relationship I could establish with them as a group, as well as with individual students. There was profanity in the scene, and I wondered if this would offend the students because of what I was learning about their religiosity.

On the first day we met, I asked my students to write about a salient reading experience. It could be something they had read recently or anytime in their lives. I just wanted to know about any reading experience that stood out in their minds. Five students wrote about reading religious texts—such as the Bible, a daily devotional book, and "Christian" novels such as the popular Left Behind series by Tim LaHaye (see Hitchcock & Ice, 2004). In talking with me about how they decide what to read and where they go to find material to read, several students made it clear that they primarily shop for books at Christian bookstores. The only male student always brought to class a copy of the Bible and kept it on his desk. Given my secularist outlook and northeastern U.S. upbringing, I wondered if southerners and Christian conservatives would be severely judgmental of Raymond for selling marijuana and for using profanity in poetry. Would they admire Raymond's literate acumen as I did? Would they value, as I did, the thoughtful responses of the other prisoners to Raymond's poetic performance of "Amethyst Rocks"?

I showed the prison-yard scene as a way of making the point that language can be a powerful means of dealing with difficult life situations. I wanted to challenge any stereotypes these future elementary school teachers might have about people who end up in prison. I wanted them to think about the stereotypes they knowingly or unknowingly had that underestimate the intelligence and creative potential of inmates, regardless of sex, race, or ethnicity. Unfortunately, at the time, I did not bring my personal history to them. I had not yet made the connection between a risky teaching decision and relevant personal experiences.

After showing the scene "Amethyst Rocks" from *Slam*, I found myself wondering what the students thought as they eagerly collected their books to move onto another education course. The next day I showed the same scene to a class of graduate students who were all veteran teachers. I was sharing with them an example of how I was using experiences from reading and viewing films in my teaching. They questioned me: Why had I waited until the end of class to show this when there was no time for discussion? I knew why. It has been my experience that students preparing to teach reading are highly anxious about being responsible for teaching children to read. They want very much to learn "the best method" to teach reading. They want to know about phonics and how to teach it. Their view of teaching reading is that it is primarily about decoding words and that it will unproblematically lead to comprehension. New teachers of reading need to learn that fluent word identification with vocabulary knowledge contributes to reading comprehension, and that comprehension and interpretation of text calls for other cognitive and affective processes. Furthermore, I think it is important that I prompt new teachers of reading to think about the social, cultural, and political contexts that affect teaching and learning to read. I thought that the scene from *Slam* was an opportunity to prompt thinking about the interrelatedness of language, knowledge, class, race, and gender.

The next time I met with my undergraduate students, I asked them to write anonymously about the scene from the movie *Slam*. I said that I was curious to know if they thought it was an educational experience and, if so, why. I admitted that I wondered if the scene was shocking or disturbing to them. I received 24 responses. I used their responses and made a "found data" poem that captured the recurrent and conflicting themes that helped me to understand my students' thinking. Found poems are, quite simply, poems constructed of language that is found and arranged, rather than of language one generates (Sullivan, 2005; see Commeyras & Kelly, 2002, for more information on found poems).

Never Been to a Prison
Reading and Writing have nothing
nothing to do with these lives.

But

through a poem
the power of words
strengthened him.
He put the gangs off.

Like

this would ever happen!
Gangs would leave him

alone because of poetry.

Once

he began speaking
people respect intellect.
Reading and writing is cool.

Too

much profanity.
Foul

How

truly powerful language can be!
He blew prisoners' minds.

Yeah...

we left class discussing
how he rhymed his way

out

out of trouble!

Out of trouble!

The process of writing this poem led me to conclude that showing students the scene from the movie *Slam* was educational. Their responses indicated that it prompted them to think beyond simple judgments. As I write this, these former students are now teachers. I wonder if they recall this event among the many that comprised their early childhood teacher education program of study. What do they think now? Did this moment of risky teaching matter? And how might it matter in relation to everything else I did to engage them in critical inquiry as readers and teachers of reading?

■ Accepting the Risks in Critical Inquiry Pedagogy

As we—Bren, Sharon, Jill Hermann-Wilmarth, and Michelle—all explored risky propositions in our classrooms, we were reminded of what we learned about ourselves, our students, and our teaching after dipping, with caution, into the waters of critical inquiry. While the physical manifestations—a quickened pulse, sweaty palms, ringing ears—of risky teaching still remind us that what we are doing is not easy, we know after our two years of sharing experiences within our small cohort of four that the risk is worth the concerns it raises. We have come to accept that when teachers challenge students to do more than recall information, risk will be inevitable.

But what is risk? In each of our classrooms, it looked and felt different. Our contexts—where we taught, who we were and are, how long we'd been teaching—all made our decisions uniquely risky. Stepping outside of our own comfort zones—bucking our personal status quo—constituted risk for each of us. We were sensitive to whatever risk any one of us took or felt. The risks were equally important. There was no hierarchy of risky teaching among us. The children's literature Bren was unsure about might be innocuous for Jill's university teaching. Departing from typical teacher–student response patterns methods might be edgy for Sharon, but for Michelle, these patterns might have been discarded long ago. What Jill risked in being open about her personal life might be too uncomfortable for Michelle. And all these contrasts could change in a year, or two, or three. What feels risky is not static; it moves backward and forward along a continuum that accounts for a multitude of factors, such as political climates and personal commitment to particular issues at particular times. What mattered to our cohort of four was that we did it. We engaged in risky teaching to learn about critical inquiry pedagogy. And we were lucky because we supported one another as each of us found the courage to teach anew. We knew we were not alone because we had one another. We had created a community that sustained us.

We took risks as teachers because, like Giussani (2001), we insisted on an education that is critical. We agree that it is our responsibility as literacy educators to invite, encourage, and lead our students to examine language and speech issues; consider multiple and contradictory viewpoints; and examine the influence of one's biography in learning about others as well as oneself. The possibility of undesirable outcomes will always be there, but, fortunately, we have experienced desirable outcomes as well. Being risk-taking teachers was easier than anticipated because we had one another. Certainly, we will continue to seek alliances with others who are willing to take risks because of our commitment to provide an education that dares to be critical.

CHAPTER 6

Ways of Working: Community Building, Responsibility, and Risk Among Teacher Researchers

When we talk in the larger group [large cohort] and then...split up into small groups of people from other cohorts and really hear how they are living their inquiry in their classrooms, [it] helps me to think about how I need to be doing things differently, or how I need to push myself. How I need to ask [the other teachers], "Why are you doing this? And what are you doing here?" Hearing [about] all of the different ways people are framing inquiry in their classrooms just helps me think about praxis in a broader sense [than] just in my own little classroom or than in my own small cohort.... That's why this group has been important—because the more people I talk to in different settings who are thinking and using a similar philosophy, the more I can blow that philosophy open for myself. (Jill Hermann-Wilmarth)

Involvement in the large cohort required a high level of commitment from its members, along with a willingness to be challenged by others, as is evident in Jill's words quoted at the beginning of this chapter. For all of the teacher researchers in this project, enacting critical inquiry pedagogy in classrooms was difficult work. Support and encouragement from others was, therefore, an integral feature of the project's design. Support involved many activities—group meetings, e-mail journaling, observations of one another's teaching, readings discussions, group data analysis, collaborative writing, and conference presentations.

As an external evaluator of this critical inquiry group, I (Kathy Roulston) listened to these teacher researchers describe their involvement in the project. They talked about the everyday difficulties of devoting sufficient time and attention to critical inquiry pedagogy and teacher research in their classrooms. Their descriptions included encounters with student resistance, structural and systemic constraints, and the personal pain of seeing one's weaknesses and shortcomings as a teacher. Novice teachers reported the additional work required by the project as especially challenging. In retrospect, however, the novice teachers spoke positively of their experiences. Across the large cohort, it seemed that the benefits of participation outweighed the difficulties they traversed. One of the beginning teachers, Ellen Elrick, commented at the end of her second year of involvement:

I would say overall it was positive, and definitely worthwhile, though there were times where I said, "Why am I doing this?" [Because] it's a lot of work, and it's...definitely new territory to me, and it's hard when you're doing anything, I think, that's new to you [because] you don't know what to expect. But I think it's been a positive, worthwhile experience. Even for just the people that I've met and formed friendships with, and that sort of thing, it's been worthwhile for that. It's also been very positive in terms of...how it's improved me as a teacher. I think I'm much further along in my...teaching development [and] growth than I would be had I just been in my classroom figuring it all by myself. This has definitely pushed me further.

For Ellen, the support of her fellow cohort members was crucial to her learning experiences of both a beginning researcher and teacher. In her statement, we glimpse some of the challenges of engaging in teacher research. It is difficult, and there are moments of doubt. Yet Ellen retrospectively counted the experience as beneficial to her professional development, and other group members said similar things. Veteran and novice teachers alike described moments of difficulty and uncertainty. Other narratives spoke to the support and encouragement received from other group members, along with moments of challenge, inspiration, and fun.

In this chapter, I provide an outsider perspective on this complex large cohort. My view is not holistic—I did not visit the teachers' classrooms; I did not attend cohort meetings on a regular basis; I was not part of each small cohort's online interactions with one another. I was an invited and interested outsider. You might think of the view I present as fragmented glimpses of the study—much like the snapshots tourists take while visiting foreign cities. Foreigners are inclined to notice what's odd, unusual, and different. What stands out to a tourist may be the very object that locals omit when giving directions to lost travelers. As I examined this project, I watched, listened, read, took notes, and pondered; my main question was, "What is going on here?" But first, let me introduce myself.

■ Introducing the External Evaluator

In January 2002, Bob Fecho and Michelle Commeyras invited me to lunch to discuss a research project that they were beginning. They asked if I would be interested in evaluating the activities of a teacher research group. Having just completed another qualitative evaluation study as part of a team project, I was keen to gain further skills in doing evaluation research. I teach qualitative research methods, and the project seemed to include opportunities for thinking about two kinds of qualitative research: (1) qualitative evaluation and (2) teacher research. As a former elementary music specialist, I have a continuing interest in teachers' work in K–12 settings, and it seemed that I could learn much from the group about emerging topics of individual and collective investigation and about the process of doing teacher research.

Some of my research interests are situated in the field of music education, and I am intrigued by the possibilities of applying qualitative research methods to research problems that music education researchers frequently use quantitative methods to investigate. My journeys in qualitative research methodologies have entailed venturing into fields of study outside of my discipline. I saw the task of evaluating the large cohort's work as another opportunity to cross disciplinary boundaries—this time, into the areas of literacy education and teacher education.

In April 2002, in Athens, Georgia, USA, I met with the large cohort, which then consisted of nine members (see Appendix A). As a junior faculty member, I was aware of and somewhat intimidated by the seniority and academic records of the senior investigators in the group. Would my work stand up to their scrutiny? As a researcher whose interests lie outside of literacy and critical inquiry pedagogy, would I be able to contribute? Could I speak in meaningful ways to all members of the group? The large cohort called on me, too, to take risks.

At this meeting I discussed the purpose of my external evaluation and possible questions of interest. Patton (2002) defines *evaluative research* as systematic inquiry that focuses on assessing the "outcomes of programs to make judgments about the program" (p. 10)—in other words, have the people involved accomplished what they set out to do? Evaluation research requires data-based judgments concerning effectiveness through systematic data collection and analysis. I explained my aim to the group in a large cohort meeting:

> You have the use of someone else to inform you of what is happening in the group. Perhaps what is working really well in one cohort...could inform another cohort. What might not be working so well?

My aim was to provide information to project participants on the organization and operation of the large cohort and to identify issues of concern and possibilities for future direction. In effect, I was presenting interim "report cards" to evaluate the large cohort's ways of working in relation to their stated goals.

In this chapter, I first describe the research methods I used for the qualitative evaluation study of the group's ways of working before briefly highlighting the key findings from the two evaluation reports. I use the research themes generated by each small cohort—community, responsibility, and risk—as a way of organizing and presenting the tensions inherent in the collaborative work that the large cohort accomplished. Specifically, I discuss the following questions:

- How did the group develop a sense of community?
- How did the group members allocate and manage responsibilities across both large and small cohorts?
- What risks were involved for teacher researchers in doing this work?

I then conclude the chapter with a short discussion of what other teacher researchers might learn from the ways in which this large cohort worked.

■ Research Design and Methods

I met with the large cohort on two occasions in 2002 to discuss my evaluation process and explore interview questions. After the first meeting, I generated a list of questions that I distributed to all group members for their comment and revision. Findings presented in the first report were based on analysis of three data sources: (1) transcripts of one- to two-hour focus group discussions with each of the three small cohorts; (2) 30 e-mails that cohort members posted to the cohort's asynchronous discussion list from February to June 2002; and (3) a transcript of talk from the large cohort's meeting conducted in April 2002 where cohort members discussed the evaluation report. While I led the focus group discussions in Athens, Eurydice Bouchereau Bauer led the focus group discussion of the Champaign, Illinois, cohort and forwarded the audiotape of that meeting to me for transcription and analysis. I used an inductive process to code and categorize data into key findings that were presented in a 53-page report in September 2002.

Data sources for the second evaluation report, submitted in September 2003, differed from the first in one respect—this time, I conducted individual interviews with all cohort members, either by telephone or face to face (these ranged in duration from 35 minutes to 2 hours with most ranging from 45–60 minutes). In my analysis, I included 250 e-mails and attachments posted to the group discussion list from July 2002 to August 2003, as well as the transcript of a large cohort meeting held in Athens in September 2002. Again, I analyzed data inductively to examine commonalities and differences in views expressed across the large cohort. I presented both reports summarizing findings of the evaluation studies to all cohort members at the completion of each academic year (2001–2002 and 2002–2003), and cohort members discussed the findings at subsequent meetings. In the next section, I report key findings from the two reports, before examining, in further detail, the themes of building a community, sharing responsibility, and taking risks.

■ The First Year of the Research Project

At the conclusion of the 2001–2002 academic year, I found that each cohort had established a strong sense of community and that they had achieved progress toward "flattening" the hierarchical relationships traditionally found in K–12/university relationships. Group members reported that cross cohort (that is, the members of the two Athens cohorts were able to meet together on multiple occasions in a "cross cohort" group) and large cohort meetings were beneficial to the work of teacher research. In particular, novice teachers and novice researchers profited from working with more experienced colleagues. Across the group, members had developed a deeper understanding of key terms (such as *praxis* and *critical inquiry pedagogy*) that were central to the project, and the organization of the small cohorts had allowed for different preferred methods of working collaboratively to develop. Overall, cohort members reported that there were many benefits for K–12 teachers and teacher educators engaging in collaborative work.

Group members also reported areas of concern. Accounts provided in interviews indicated that comfortable peer relationships were not yet fully developed across the large cohort, and group members had different perceptions of the levels of research-related activity for which each member was responsible. At this point in the project, full-time faculty members took on the primary organizational responsibilities within the large cohort. Some group members rarely engaged in certain activities—such as use of e-mail for discussion purposes among groups. Group members commonly reported structural difficulties in both K–12 and university contexts that made engaging in inquiry-based work difficult. For example, one of the K–12 teachers, Bren Daniell, spoke of the pressures of taking classroom time for critical inquiry pedagogy in addition to adequately preparing her students for state-mandated testing. Likewise, teacher educators Bob and Michelle talked about the challenges of creating the necessary community to enact critical inquiry pedagogy in semester-long undergraduate courses. Members of the group also commented that a concerted effort would have to be made to fully involve and support newcomers to the project in the second year.

■ The Second Year of the Research Project

At the conclusion of the second year of the project, the teacher researchers described their involvement in the university–school partnership as productive. The nested structure of the cohorts had provided an environment that facilitated teacher research, and strong support and mentoring of novice teachers was evident. K–12 teachers and teacher educators provided accounts of changes in personal understanding and professional growth in their classroom practice. Over the course of the second year of the project, K–12 teachers had taken on new roles and responsibilities within the large cohort. All members had participated in conference presentations and were making progress in writing reports of their work.

Participants identified issues for further discussion, including their questions related to research methods, differing expectations of publishing outcomes from the study, decision making around identifying settings for meetings of the large cohort, and expectations for members' participation in future work. Other questions pertained to how inquiry-based work might be most effectively facilitated in the face of structural constraints in K–12 and university settings and to how sustained focus and energy might be maintained in teacher research projects over lengthy periods of time.

Overall, findings from both reports indicated the potential to effect change in teachers' practices through a teacher research group with a central focus on critical inquiry pedagogy. Working with a group pushed teachers to consider their actions and implement changes in their everyday work. Jennifer Aaron, for example, described how the teacher researchers' focus on critical inquiry pedagogy disrupted her established routines as a mid-career teacher:

> You get into that routine and you have that lesson that works well, and so you do that lesson, and it gets done again each year—year after year. But when you involve critical inquiry, there are all these things that happen.... If I was doing this alone, I think after the second or third month, I'd say, "OK, nevermind...[I] don't want to go off on any more tangents." But knowing...others are having to figure it out also or have figured it out and have suggestions of what I can do is what...gets me through.

Indeed, collaborative action by these teachers in K–12 and university settings provided opportunities to overcome the traditional theory–practice divide between teachers and educational researchers because all were involved in investigations of their praxis. Andrea Pintaone-Hernandez, a second-grade teacher, summed up her experience in the K–12/university partnership as follows:

> I think [the K–12/university partnership has] been very easy, and I think that the university people that have been involved with the project have been engaged as much as the K–12 teachers have. It hasn't been a situation where I've felt like the university professors had...finished learning,

they were experts on critical inquiry, and they were done—this was for [K–12 teachers]. I feel like we've all learned so much and grown so much in this project, that those distinctions aren't even clear most of the time.

As an endpoint, Andrea's description encompasses much that was hoped for in outcomes of the study—engagement, growth, and learning through the collaborative effort of university and K–12 educators. It sounds easy, but was it?

■ Building a Community of Teacher Researchers

The large cohort involved multiple layers of complexity in that it involved small cohorts (from two states in the United States) nested within a large cohort and individuals from multiple K–12 and higher education settings. Given this complexity, how was a sense of community developed over time that supported the work of each individual? The teacher researchers interacted in a number of ways—in small-cohort, cross-cohort, and large-cohort meetings and informal settings. I will describe each venue in more detail in the following section.

Interaction Within and Among Small Cohorts

Members of each cohort met with one another in homes, schools, restaurants, and coffeehouses for several hours on a monthly basis. Cohort members reported these meetings as less regular in the second year of the project as the focus of the group's activities changed from research design and data collection to data analysis and presentation of findings. In the first year of the project, the responsibility and risk-taking cohorts in Athens were able to meet together on two occasions for cross-cohort activities. Some members reported that they would have liked more of these cross-cohort meetings. Although the large cohort met for only two days in the first year of the project, meetings became more frequent in the second year. These full-group meetings involved discussion and data analysis, presentations at the National Council of Teachers of English (NCTE) conference in Atlanta, Georgia, and the Qualitative Interest Group (QUIG) Conference in Athens, and a writing retreat in Nashville, Tennessee, USA. One outcome of the large-cohort meetings was the organization of more social events, which enabled members to get to know one another in casual settings.

Interviews with the teacher researchers over the course of the project show that it took time for the large cohort to develop the kind of community that Jill described in the excerpt at the beginning of this chapter.

Although all members spoke of deriving much from hearing others' views at large-cohort meetings, even after the first year, individuals still did not know one another well. For example, Bob commented at the completion of the first year:

> I think in some ways, the large cohort is only just now starting to coalesce. What I've liked about [the large-cohort meetings is] sometimes we do other things...we do look at data, and you get other people's views on your data.... When we get into a larger cohort, then the discussion seems to broaden.... [yet] On the other hand, I don't always remember who everybody is.... But it doesn't have the same level of comfort at first, and it's only now, I think, starting to approach that.

This passage demonstrates some of the complex dynamics of the large cohort interactions. The teacher researchers gained much from the multiple perspectives and expanded discussions presented by other group members at large-cohort meetings.

Nonetheless, it took time for some members to feel comfortable sharing their views within the large cohort, and cohort members generally viewed the geographical distance between the Champaign cohort and Athens cohorts as a barrier to the development of peer relationships across groups. At the completion of the first year, members sometimes failed during focus group discussions to remember other members' names or commented that they had little knowledge of others' research interests and classrooms. By the end of the second year, members of the large cohort had accomplished much in terms of developing relationships with one another—but some individuals still expressed discomfort with taking risks within the large cohort. This contrasted with accounts of small-cohort interaction, in which an environment of support for risk taking was more rapidly established. In the following section, I address the formation of community within and across cohorts in further detail.

Developing a Risk-Taking Community in a Teacher Research Group

In Athens, the responsibility- and risk-taking cohorts involved members who were known to one another prior to the project. Sharon Dowling Cox, a speech–language pathologist, described how the sense of community in her small cohort was both preestablished when she joined the project in the second year and developed further through her collaborative work.

I think we worked well together because of the relationships that we previously had.... I was a costudent [in university course work] with Jill before. Michelle [was our] former professor, and then Bren was my child's teacher. We had history, and I felt a certain comfort level in taking risks and shar[ing] my ideas about who I am and what I do. And it's having somebody that you know already, I think, it makes taking those risks less...daunting, and then you have somebody else to celebrate the small successes with. It builds a comforting anchor on what could otherwise be an isolating journey...[to have other teachers] to give me feedback. I also learned about their work. Listening to their presentations, their writing, the discussions that we had...broadened my view of teachers' perspectives in university settings, as well as [the] elementary classroom.... I benefited tremendously from their view into my work because they offered me a fresh perspective, and it made a very positive impact on my teaching strategies and my thinking about student learning.

For Sharon, the preestablished relationships she had with her small-cohort members provided an environment of safety and support for her to take risks. The supportive environment developed in her small cohort offered her an anchor from which she could begin her own voyage as a teacher researcher.

The formation of group cohesiveness in the Champaign cohort developed along a somewhat different path than did the Athens cohorts. In Champaign, Eurydice had taken a new position at another university, and her engagement with others in the project entailed fostering new relationships, one of which was with her daughter's teacher. In the focus group discussion at the completion of the first year of the project, Eurydice commented:

When working with...Ellen, initially, I thought, "Oh my God, she used to be [my daughter's] teacher. How's this going to work? Can we be peers, and collegial, and all these different things, without her thinking of me as a parent, or my thinking of her as [my daughter's] teacher?"

Ellen, too, found the parent–teacher relationship described by Eurydice initially disconcerting. Speaking to Eurydice at the same focus group, Ellen reflected on her initial reaction to driving with Eurydice, Amanda Siegel, and Eurydice's daughter to Georgia from Illinois for a large-cohort meeting: "Do you remember that car trip? OK, you're in the car with a parent, and a student. Are you nuts?" However, all members of the Champaign cohort spoke of how the long trips to meetings in Georgia inevitably strengthened relationships within the group. For example, Amanda described the collegiality developed through many hours spent traveling together:

[We made] several trips to Georgia…[we spent] 15 hours in the car together. You do a whole lot of talking—both on the professional, academic, and personal level. So I think because we've made those sorts of connections, we've really been able to expose ourselves and get out of our safety zones.

As Amanda previously reported, personal connections that facilitated risk taking were first formed in small cohorts, and by the completion of the second year, the large cohort had developed a stronger sense of community. Personal and professional ties developed through members' collaborative work at meetings, conference presentations, and participation in a writing retreat and social activities. Whereas the large-cohort meetings provided members with inspiration and a sense of excitement about the project, the small-cohort meetings provided the environment that sustained the continued work of doing teacher research.

The Challenge of Geographical Distances in Building a Sense of Community

Over the two-year period of the project, however, the large cohort made little progress in treating the geographical distance between cohorts as other than a barrier. For the group, the *Tyranny of Distance*—a term coined by the Australian historian Geoffrey Blainey (1982)—interfered with the development of cross-cohort connections. Eurydice explained:

It is sad to say, but we didn't focus on the possible benefit to looking at teachers across two states…. No one said, "That's not the way we envisioned it, but what are the benefits we could get from this?" And that was really disturbing to me, and, I think, to our group. I know within our small [cohort] we talked about it. But I must say, things did improve as the project continued.

Geographical distance between the Athens and Champaign cohorts was problematic for two reasons. First, the cost of assembling all members of the group in either state was prohibitive of planning for large-cohort meetings. This necessitated that the majority of meetings take place in Athens. Second, members of the Champaign cohort spent considerably more time traveling to and from meetings than other members. Although travel time was reported as assisting in the building of warm and collegial relationships, it also was lengthy, tiresome, and costly for the Champaign cohort because extra time was necessary to devote to participation in the project.

Flattening Hierarchies Among K–12 Teachers and Teacher Educators

As I discussed earlier, the "flattening of traditional hierarchies" between K–12 teachers and teacher educators was a continual goal of the large cohort. In the first year of the project, some members commented that the positions held by the lead investigators (i.e., Michelle, Eurydice, and Bob) intimidated them. Becoming aware of this was something of a revelation to these teacher educators. For example, Michelle, after describing an incident with an undergraduate student to her small cohort, expressed surprise when one of the cohort members pointed out that her position could be seen as "intimidating" by students, saying, "It's such a shock to find out that somebody is intimidated by me. I had no idea." The intimidation K–12 teachers feel with respect to teacher educators was not confined to undergraduate students, however. For example, at the completion of the first year, two teachers commented about their initial unease with relating to teacher educators as "colleagues" rather than as university professors and teachers:

Bren: It was kind of a stretch for me [laughter] to accept her as someone I could call "Michelle," instead of "Dr. Commeyras."

Andrea: It was scary for me to have Bob, "Mr. [Critical] Inquiry," come and look [laughter], [at] my classroom.

Hope Vaughn commented that the composition of the large cohort was helpful in alleviating these feelings of intimidation:

I think the fact that there are more...K–12 teachers in the group [large cohort] brings a certain comfort to [being involved]; that if it were predominantly university professors and a few K–12 teachers—that comfort wouldn't be there. Because there's an intimidation, I think, between [K–12] teachers and [university] professors, and probably because there is more of us [K–12 teachers], it helps us to feel like we've got more of a voice and.... I wouldn't have felt comfortable because I have...no research experience. I'm a novice teacher, and then you [work] with [a researcher] who's being cited.

By the completion of the project, accounts of intimidation such as these were mostly absent from interview data. Some members, however, still spoke of being intimidated by the act of research. One K–12 teacher, for example, commented at the end of the second year, "I'm still nervous and intimidated with the process, and so until I just let go of my intimidation, I don't know that it'll be very successful for me." Comments such as these suggest the need for a long-term view of university–school partnerships. The time and professional support required for practitioners to develop the skills and knowledge necessary to conduct quality investigations of their praxis is likely to be much longer than research projects in which university researchers visit schools for short periods of time before exiting with data in hand.

Learning Through Diversity

Teachers described the diverse large- and small-cohort groupings as being beneficial in providing views from beyond their respective classrooms. Jennifer, for example, commented on how the composition of her small cohort had given her access to differing perspectives unavailable to her in a local school setting:

> It's been very helpful to have people from different grade levels [in my cohort]. We have a college [teacher], a high school–middle school [teacher], and a lower-grades elementary [teacher]. And because I'm dealing with fifth grade, I [fit] into the middle, and that has been really nice.... I mean we're all coming at it from very different viewpoints, and so [other members of my small cohort] notice things that I would have never caught on to.

To summarize, members reported the development of a strong sense of community within each small cohort. Across the large cohort, this was slower to develop because the large cohort simply did not meet as often due to the distance among small cohorts. While, initially, some members were intimidated by the research expertise and experience that other members brought to the group, these feelings appeared to dissipate over the course of the project. Participants also spoke of the benefits that they experienced from hearing the different perspectives others offered in diverse cohort groupings.

Throughout the project, cohort members made much progress in working together across the boundaries that separate schools, districts, and states. Along with the development of community was a concurrent taking on of responsibility for the cohort's activities by individual cohort members. I turn now to the topic of how sharing responsibility was accomplished.

■ Sharing Responsibility Among the Large Cohort

At first, the involvement of novice teachers *and* novice researchers in the large cohort caused some tension with regard to the stated goal of "flattening the hierarchy" between K–12 teachers and teacher educators. In the following sections, I present the grant writers'—Eurydice, Michelle, and Bob—and

K–12 teachers' views on the topic of shared responsibility for the group's collaborative efforts.

The Lead Investigators' Views of Sharing Responsibility

Although the grant writers' intent was to provide greater space for all cohort members to participate in other aspects of research (such as development of conference proposals and presentations), this did not immediately occur. This is exemplified by the teacher educators' approach to the call for proposals for a qualitative research conference in May 2002. Bob explained this further:

> [I]t would be real easy for [the grant writers] just to sit down and say, "Well, QUIG proposal, well, let's write a proposal." But we try not to do that; we try to send it out to the big group. Now, we don't always get a lot of response from the group. But at least we're trying to put it out there. And we've recognized the fact that...there are probably some teachers in our group who have no idea what QUIG is, so even asking, "So...what's that?" So, they're not going to write a proposal because they have to figure out what it is. But...we also feel we need to...let people know that we'll write it as a group, we'll share these thoughts. But getting out of that habit, too, of even just thinking to do that.... Because at first, at the first meetings like Michelle and I would get together before a large-cohort meeting and say, "Well, one of us has to plan it." And finally I said, "Well, I'll tell you what, why doesn't my group plan one of these meetings? And then your group plans one of the meetings?".... We've been trying to share the load.

In the first year of the project, the lead investigators (Michelle, Eurydice, and Bob) acknowledged that some teachers might not have the knowledge, skills, nor time to directly contribute to other research-related activities (e.g., writing conference proposals and presenting). The lead investigators were, however, explicit in defining one of the purposes of the large cohort working with others to develop new skills. Eurydice commented:

> All of us were inexperienced at one time, and it's not as if you're out there totally on your own. We're willing to provide, you know, some assistance. But if it's always that...Bob, Eurydice, and Michelle always take care of everything, [then], in a sense,...the learning that could take place is minimized.

Eurydice's words illustrate the lead investigators' views of wanting to encourage K–12 teachers and novice researchers to participate and take responsibility for multiple aspects of doing teacher research. For all cohort members, opportunity knocked. Did doors open?

K–12 Teachers' Views of Taking Responsibility in the Teacher Research Group

Just as a cautious homeowner might keep the security chain latched prior to opening the door fully, teachers did not necessarily take up these [leadership] opportunities immediately. For example, one teacher stated that she was "not a speaker," and although she was willing to attend a conference (which was, for her, a new experience), she would not participate in an oral presentation. Another respondent wrote to the listserv, "I have never done anything like that [a conference presentation] before or even watched a professional presentation to even know what to do or where to start. If I can help in the background work, I will." This teacher stated in her focus group discussion, "There [are] some things I just don't know how to do yet, so to take on that part of the leadership would be [a] really hard thing to do."

Yet other teacher researchers eagerly embraced opportunities to take on other roles within the large cohort. For example, Jill, a preservice teacher educator, took a lead role in preparing her small cohort's presentation for one conference by writing a script performed by the members of her small cohort. Hope sent via e-mail the following message to the large cohort in May 2002:

> I'm game for any proposals, presentations, conferences, etc., and I will be glad to do whatever is necessary. My only concern is that I am unfamiliar with all of the groups except for NCTE. I might need a little assistance as to how to direct any writing.

The topic of cohort members taking on more responsibility within the group provided the source of some lively discussion at a large-group meeting in late 2002, and one year later it was evident that teacher researchers had taken on new tasks.

Taking on New Responsibilities

After two years, all cohort members had contributed to one another's topics through group data analysis and discussion, and all had been involved in conference presentations. These presentations included annual meetings of the NCTE in Atlanta in 2002 and of the QUIG in Athens in 2003. Other members had contributed to the writing of a successful proposal for $5,000 of further funding from the International Reading Association. All members reported that the conference presentations had been successful events, although some spoke of experiencing a good deal of preconference anxiety. Speaking of her involvement in conference presentations, Ellen, for example, commented, "that's been pretty exciting. I know the first one, NCTE, was very nerve-racking, and I was just a ball of nerves...the week before."

Despite the initial discomfort about presentations that Ellen and other cohort members described, they spoke positively about the outcomes of taking on new tasks and responsibilities within the various cohorts. For example, Hope spoke of gaining a broader view of her small cohort's part in the large-cohort structure through the conference presentations:

> We did a presentation as the [large cohort], and it was really interesting because each individual had a part that became part of his or her small cohort, and then [the presentation] all came together as whole. So there were [three small cohorts], and it was interesting how fluid it was.... So it just was interesting how it all worked out.

Elizabeth Hogan also described the value of her involvement in presenting the large cohort's work at a conference. In one presentation, Elizabeth provided videotaped interaction from her high school classroom to demonstrate a variation of the process of descriptive review—a process of reviewing data that the large cohort used that was derived from the work of Carini (2001). Concerning this presentation, Elizabeth commented:

> And so, even going through all of that with my small cohort again, I got so much feedback and was able to see things in my students that I hadn't seen before, which probably affected our whole classroom interaction after that.... I was grateful just to have that experience because I had all this feedback from, you know, [teachers] all over the country on my practice and what was going on with my students.

As both of these excerpts indicate, the presentations helped to create a sense of community and worth, even though some members described stress and anxiety prior to the events.

Bob provided an overview of the role of the conference presentations within the larger context of the large cohort's work; he commented that the presentations assisted cohort members to "make some sense" of their research project, gain a view of the large cohort's project, and work toward framing a concrete outcome—in this case, the book you are now reading.

> NCTE was followed by QUIG, and they were both different; it forced...all of us, to...get a handle on things, and not put this [work] off, and not just...talk about it continually, which can sometimes happen in groups such as this because it's fun talking. It forced us to really get something [done]. Getting the grant done, to a certain extent, was the same thing; it sort of forced us to

say, well, what is it that we're doing that we can put on paper to [describe the project to] someone else? So I think both of those presentations weren't going to set the world on fire; on the other hand, in terms of the group's [large cohort's] process, [the presentations] were fabulous, because again, I think they helped everybody make some sense [of our research]. They helped all of us start seeing the larger picture.

To sum up, then, cohort members challenged one another to take responsibility for learning new skills—both as teachers and researchers. They did not immediately accept this challenge; yet, by the completion of the project, all cohort members had demonstrated their commitment by participating in conferences and signaled their continued interest in the completion of this book. Over the course of the second year of the project, members of the large cohort had taken responsibility for a greater variety of activities. These activities included the organization of social activities during large-cohort meetings, leading conference presentations, reporting group activities to the listserv, and organizing chapter writing.

It seems then that when teacher educators and K–12 teachers are willing to work together, it is possible to flatten some of the traditional hierarchies. This process is unlikely to occur without effort from all who are involved. First, those who work in universities must actively create spaces for K–12 teachers to take on further responsibility. They must actively let go of responsibilities and provide the requisite support for those willing to take on new tasks. Second, those who initiate teacher research groups must allow cohort members to develop skills and accept different responsibilities over time, because such change will not immediately occur. Third, taking on more responsibility involves risk taking—in a community where trust and support are firmly established. In the next section, I further explore these teacher researchers' descriptions of the risks they took and their personal and professional outcomes.

■ Teachers Taking Risks With Critical Inquiry Pedagogy

Data analysis from the evaluation study suggests that teachers who take on critical inquiry pedagogy to examine tough issues and difficult questions must be risk takers and able to examine their frailties, shortcomings, and humanness in order to reflect in meaningful ways. This characteristic was described in interview accounts from teachers across the large cohort—whether novice or veteran, K–12 teachers or teacher educators.

In participating in the project, all cohort members took on *more*, and, possibly, *more difficult* work. This quantitative and qualitative change in workload was most apparent in novice teachers' descriptions, as they spoke of entering the project with limited knowledge about how to engage in teacher research; yet they learned much from participating. This learning encompassed gaining a wider view and understanding of the field of education—through hard work, uncertainty, and sometimes emotional discomfort. Amanda commented:

> [Involvement in the project has] given me a much broader sense and a better picture of the world of education. When I first joined this group, I had no idea what I was getting into. Ellen came to me and asked me if I wanted to join her and another professor who were reading a book together and kind of discussing how it affected them in the classroom. And I thought, "Sure, why not? I'd like to keep up with what's current in education and talk about educational issues together with somebody." And it ended up being a [much] bigger project than I had ever first assumed. That there were, at the time, six other people, but now it's an even a larger group that's creating this, all this research and analysis.... It's really given me a challenge and it feels really good to be a part of this challenge. I feel much more confident in who I am as a teacher, and to know that there [are] other teachers out there that are struggling and learning during their first year of teaching, which continues for all the way up into 20-plus years of teaching.

Novice teachers reported that the extra demands of the project's workload were challenging; these novice teachers were, at the same time, struggling with the day-to-day demands of learning how to manage a myriad of aspects of their work.

Novice Teachers' Views on the Outcomes of Their Involvement in a Teacher Research Project

For novice teachers, the risk of participating in a project that led to more hard work and questioning also resulted in the satisfaction of personal and professional growth. Andrea, for example, expressed growing self-assurance and confidence in her abilities as a teacher practicing inquiry pedagogy:

> I think for my [teaching] practice, this project has given me confidence to trust some of my instincts about inquiry and to trust the process. [It's helped me to work on] allowing students to engage in what they're really interested in, and being encouraging and supportive without squashing whatever interest they have. So I think it's meant confidence for me.

Involvement in the large cohort provided encouragement to Hope to counter the growing discouragement and despair she reported experiencing in her second and third years of teaching. Hope reported, at the completion of the second year of research, that had she "not had the Spencer Group, I think I would be leaving education for good." While Hope took a break from teaching to care for her newborn twins in 2003, she expected to return to teaching at a future time and spoke positively of her experience with the large cohort.

Amanda also chose not to return to teaching at the beginning of the 2003–2004 school year. In my interview with her in May 2003, she had spoken very positively about her involvement in the large cohort and wanted to continue doing this type of work. In spite of, or perhaps because of, this positive account of doing teacher research, she chose to pursue full-time graduate studies in 2004. Below, Amanda pondered on her future as a teacher researcher.

Kathy: Do you see yourself continuing in this kind of work?

Amanda: I do want to continue with research. I'd like to say that I would do this anyway without a group. That I'd analyze my teaching this much, and collect this much data, and look over myself, and think that hard about what I am and who I am as a teacher. But it's really hard to do that on your own, without a support group, either backing you up, inspiring you, or just keeping the deadline on you. So to be a part of a group that keeps up with you and is so supportive makes your research and your data collection that much more valuable.

Along with the support of one's colleagues, as mentioned earlier, it appears likely that accountability to other cohort members was an important factor in ensuring that individuals continued their involvement in the project. Other teacher researchers indirectly have discussed this topic.

The Significance of Being Responsible to Others in the Large Cohort

Cohort members spoke about the importance and value of mutually supporting and prodding one another. This support and encouragement of one another for doing the work of teacher research was a crucial component of continuing the work of being a critical inquirer in the classroom. Hope, for example, commented on this aspect at a large-cohort meeting:

> Being able to have this group to talk to or just to know that you're out there and that they expect something of me has definitely helped encourage me when it would have been easy to do what everybody else at school was doing, or to use the book that they're handing you to do. I think it's sort of encouraged me to do more than that.

As Jennifer mentioned earlier, "knowing others are having to figure it out also or have figured it out and have suggestions" helped her continue doing the work of critical inquiry pedagogy. It seems then that the nested cohort structure served a dual purpose: First, the large cohort played a supportive role for members, creating a safe place for taking risks and doing things differently. Second, the large cohort played a monitoring role in that cohort members were accountable to one another to complete tasks and for continued project participation.

Time Requirements for Reflective Practice

All cohort members mentioned "time" as a problematic issue for both engaging in critical inquiry pedagogy in the classroom and undertaking the research-related tasks of reading, data collection, data analysis, and writing. With relation to teaching, Sharon commented:

> This kind of teaching demands more time to plan; it takes more time to reflect, you have to read, and then talking about it is important, too. So reflective practice takes time. I think critical inquiry takes a lot of time, in that it's sustained over time, so you have to struggle with managing the time in addition to balancing everything else that goes on in your daily life.

Cohort members in all settings described not having enough time to effectively implement critical inquiry pedagogy in their classrooms. For example, teacher educator Michelle pondered whether lack of time within a 15-week course partially was responsible for the difficulties that she had encountered with her students' responses to course assignments and assessment.

> I mean, I guess, I shook [the preservice teachers] up...as far as...their assumptions about what school is and about assessment. There are different ways of doing assessment, but perhaps I was not very successful...bringing the students into some sort of process of thinking about all of that. And part of that is you just don't have time. We don't have time to examine everything. I mean a lot of this metaanalysis that is probably part of critical inquiry pedagogy takes a lot of time, and there really isn't enough time with students to delve into all the sorts of things that you feel responsible to do in the course.

The spiral of reflective action required of teacher researchers was both encompassed and bounded by the constraints of the 24-hour day. Cohort members described a lack of time for pursuing teaching from a critical inquiry pedagogy perspective as well as insufficient time for the reading, writing, and reflection that is required to do research.

Veteran Teachers' Views on Outcomes of the Project

Like beginning teachers, veteran teachers reported satisfaction in their personal and professional growth as an outcome of the project. Elizabeth and Bren, however, commented that the reflection, introspection, and pushing beyond personal boundaries that the project required also had brought about painful feelings of doubt and confusion. In summing up the "twofold" outcome of the project for herself, Elizabeth commented:

> [The project] has impacted my classroom. I feel like I am very human with my students. I was kind of moving towards this, in the past, but I think I've moved closer. So I think that is one way it's impacted me and...has added another layer to my classroom, one that is really genuine. And then, on a personal level, too, it's just been very exciting...for veteran teachers, and for me in particular.... Although it was hard, it brought up layers of complexity and doubt that weren't there before. And it also, I think, could keep me teaching for a few [more] years. I will miss the project.

Bren, too, summed up her experience as both "painful" and "positive":

> Things that I have done, such as the presentations that I didn't enjoy doing, were painful. Like I said before, having a great deal of introspection and looking back over and coming to terms with some other personal issues was kind of painful. The thing that was very positive is the support that I got; I think that the method [of critical inquiry pedagogy] that I'm using to teach now is much more beneficial. I've seen, for the past two years, that the students do well on their reading tests without all the skill and drill. They enjoy talking. I've had more conversations going on among students and between students and me. It's more personal. So I think all the positive...changes have been directly related to participating in this group. [Because] honestly I don't know, if I'd taken a class on it...I don't know if I would have gone through the trouble of changing my whole [teaching] method unless I had...to do it this way, or try it this way.... It pushed me to do something much more beneficial...for the students. I hope, especially in light of [September 11, 2001], I've become more...conscious of all the hate that's out there. This seems to be a way...of opening up people's minds and building tolerance, and it seems so crucial [to me as a teacher].

First, this large cohort's focus on critical inquiry pedagogy provides a path of resistance for teachers wanting to work against the dominant discourses of teaching in K–12 and university settings. Bradbury and Reason (2001) argue that action-oriented researchers can intentionally repattern their realities through "participative inquiry" (p. 449) at an individual, group, and community level. The teacher educators and K–12 teachers in this project chose to work together in participatory ways that opened spaces for new dialogue about teaching, research, and personal growth.

Hopkins (2002) has proposed that schools might benefit from "networks," or groups of teacher researchers, who work to reculture schools, promote effective school reform, and support innovation. Data from the present chapter indicate that the activities of the large cohort, or to use Hopkins' term, *network*, did result in profound personal and professional changes for the teachers involved. Such change, on a widespread basis, may be one way to reculture schooling. In comparing the work of the authors of this book with the criteria for an effective network that Hopkins proposed, one finds that all conditions appear to have been met by the large cohort. Hopkins identifies six conditions for a network to be effective:

1. consistency of values and focus;
2. clarity of structure;
3. knowledge creation, utilization, and transfer;
4. rewards related to learning;
5. dispersed leadership and empowerment; and
6. adequate resources. (pp. 191–192)

While this list is useful conceptually in thinking about the kinds of conditions that are necessary for the development of effective professional networks, it belies the complexity involved in establishing networks both in and across institutions. Because my examination did not pursue the question of how the large-cohort members' colleagues in school and university communities see and take up their work, there is no way of knowing how this work contributes to a wider "reculturing" of schooling that Hopkins suggests. Research examining the different structures that are possible for the conduct of teacher research and how different organizational arrangements result in different kinds of outcomes for teachers and schools is undoubtedly worthy of further study.

Second, in addition to providing paths of resistance against dominant discourses of school, the use of qualitative and critical research methods by these researchers resists the current wave of educational research that objectifies participants and seeks to find unitary truths. As demonstrated by the large cohort, and described in this book, qualitative methods allow for the representation of multiple experiences, partial tellings in multivocal, sometimes dissonant, texts that speak for individual experiences that often resist classification, categorization, and a monolithic truth. Such writing requires self-reflection and courage, and, in this chapter, I have offered some insight into how this large cohort's ways of working enabled its members to work with critical inquiry pedagogy in their classrooms. Through the discussion of the processes, benefits, and tensions that this large cohort experienced, I hope to have shown the reader possible ways to produce the texts that, in many ways, resemble the autoethnographic writings that promote "self-understanding and ethical discussion" used by researchers such as Ellis and Bochner (2000, p. 748). The present project takes us beyond understanding and discussion, however, in that these researchers seek change for themselves and others. This change is the kind of transformation proposed by Bradbury and Reason (2001).

The reporting of educational research is necessarily partial and incomplete —incapable of telling the whole story. This chapter is no exception and provides points of reflection on the three themes of community building, taking responsibility, and risky teaching central to the presentation of the large cohort's work—rather than a comprehensive list of steps for other teacher researchers to follow. Nevertheless, in providing these glimpses into one group's ways of working, I hope to inspire others to learn from their experiences and apply this learning in active ways with others—teachers, researchers, and students—in other, local (and, perhaps, global) contexts. Rather than endlessly repeat what we have done in the past as teachers and researchers, I hope that we will continue to reflect on our own and others' practice, and in so doing, we, too, might change and grow—planning different ways of working for tomorrow.

And what of the external evaluator—did I change? In fact, inspired by this group's example, I found a small group of music teachers with whom to discuss and enact teacher research. We have just begun to write and share our stories.

I would like to thank the members of the large cohort for their openness in their conversations and interviews with me as well as providing comments and suggestions that have assisted me in revising earlier versions of this chapter.

CHAPTER 7

Getting Down to It:
The Possibilities
of Critical Inquiry

Is this [critical inquiry] for all teachers? I am not convinced it is...because it is complex, because it is difficult to do, because you have to bring in a willingness to be flexible, to be open, to care about what goes on in the lives of your students. I know I want to...[contribute] and I'd like to think that all teachers are like that, but my experience in teaching is that not all teachers are like that. (Bob Fecho)

As Bob suggested at a meeting of our large cohort in Athens, educators —novice and veteran, K–12 and university—must have an inclination to do critical inquiry research prior to involving themselves in a project such as this. Although the thought and action of looking closely at one's practice can prove beneficial to teachers of all stripes and frequently can result in engaged student learning as well as professional growth for the teacher, it is definitely not a quick fix. Rather, critical inquiry requires a complex and sustained effort, one that requires contributions of time, thought, self-revelation, and collaborative spirit.

Eurydice Bouchereau Bauer further described our experience:

There isn't a series of steps you exactly take, but we [in the large cohort] can say that in taking this stance...you have to create space, reflect, and to look at yourself critically. And in that, maybe you start looking at your [students] in similar kinds of ways.

In opposition to the hurry up, no-huddle offense—a style of U.S. football that keeps the ball active, but leaves little time for deliberation—of most modern classrooms frantically trying to teach according to and keep pace with mandated and over-specified curricula, critical inquiry requires patience and introspection on the part of all involved for understanding to evolve and opportunity to occur.

For each of us in the large cohort, a key component in this experience was how we considered the different perspectives of small- and large-cohort members. By revisiting Bakhtin's (1981) premise, we are reminded that educators cannot ignore heteroglossia, those opposing tensions that serve to sustain a thriving language classroom or any functioning community (Pintaone-Hernandez, 2002). If we structure and stylize our inquiry communities to align only with centripetal forces, we are ignoring the ways all speakers represent themselves through speech (Bakhtin, 1981), that is, the unique voices of ourselves and our students. Yet to cater only to the needs of individuals is to condemn ourselves to our petty fiefdoms, never linking to the greater possibilities beyond us.

Taking the time to reflect, to call into question, and to gather perspectives from all members of the group placed our community in opposition to the current U.S. federal administration's policies that attempt to simplify and quantify education by narrowing educators' practices to what is found on standardized tests and sanctioned by a narrow definition of what counts as scientific evidence. We do not want to avoid educational accountability; instead, we argue for increased accountability and professional responsibility, which can happen only when teachers and teacher researchers have ways to take risks and evaluate those risks within their classrooms and within a community of other educators who are also reflective practitioners.

As we reflect on our experience with critical inquiry and critical inquiry pedagogy, we acknowledge, and even revel in the acceptance, that we do not have the definitive word on what each term entails. Instead, we hold, albeit gingerly, a keener understanding of the nuanced elements of critical inquiry and critical pedagogy across various classrooms. We recognize that "the place from which we speak plays an important role in determining what we say" (Holquist, 1986, p. x). In this chapter, we will present (a) the themes that emerged from our collaborative inquiry to reflect on the process of our nested critical inquiry groups; (b) the structures we had in place that allowed the process to function; (c) the insights we gained about critical inquiry; and (d) the implications for teacher educators and researchers, K–12 teachers, and education stakeholders in general.

■ One Framework for Collaborative Research

The work of our critical inquiry community manifested itself in many ways, but we came to two broad understandings through that work. The first of these concerns what we learned about critically inquiring as a K–12 research community; the second of these involves what we came to understand about the role of critical inquiry in literacy classrooms. We will take up the second issue in the next section, but toward the first issue, we were particularly engaged in the understanding of leveling the playing field; having time for, opportunities for, and expectations of reflection; transacting as colleagues; involving observation in the third person; and making an investment in critical inquiry.

Leveling the Playing Field

Our experience researching together differed in several ways from other research that teachers and university faculty conduct when working as a team.

Perhaps the most blatant experience was the attempt to change the relationship between K–12 teachers and teacher educators. Typically, university professors gain entrance into a school and then proceed to collect data, or, if the work is collaborative, the teacher and professor collect data together, but the data is gathered solely in the teacher's classroom and never in that of the professor. As Eurydice noted, "usually you don't have the classroom teachers in a position where they can critique the university professors."

Our framework represented a departure from the way teachers may respond to doing research: The hierarchy was flattened substantially when the classroom teachers began to see themselves as coresearchers rather than subjects to be studied or novices to be mentored. Our framework puts the classroom teachers in a position of power over their practice and places the university researchers in a position in which they are forced to look at their classroom practice, to evaluate and test what is done in the classroom and whether or not students are learning. The underlying belief is that we all have practices from which we can learn and contribute to these community understandings. Furthermore, this approach to collaborative research embraces Bakhtin's (1981) centrifugal and centripetal forces, in which varied voices, roles, and agendas comingle with local, state, and national agendas, creating a far more integrative experience. As Amanda Siegel commented, "I don't feel that this is just teacher research. There really is an entire experience in it, so there is more to it than just the data we collected."

Having Time for, Opportunities for, and Expectations of Reflection

A pervasive stereotype in education is that teachers are resistant to professional development. Our experience tells us that it's not professional development per se that teachers resist; instead, they resist professional development that belittles them, infantilizes them, and is done on the cheap and the quick. The truth is that many teachers are yearning for professional development opportunities that are intellectually stimulating and empowering. The unique organization of our critical inquiry cohort created such a sustained professional development opportunity for all involved. As Elizabeth Hogan noted:

> There isn't that much space within most school buildings to be reflective, and so this group offers a space to do that...so it also can kind of shift your

perspective in terms of looking at yourself as a classroom teacher and an intellectual, which is not nurtured anywhere in the school system.

The K–12/university structure created two-way mentoring—an invigorating component for novices and veterans alike. Research on adult learners (Daines, Daines, & Graham, 1993; Knowles, 1980) has found that adults prefer learning situations that show respect for the individual learner, promote their positive self-esteem, capitalize on their experience, and allow choice and self-direction—all of which take time and consideration.

The critical inquiry framework proved especially ideal for us because we experienced much of what this research on adult learning found to be essential for stimulating learning in adult classrooms. While the veteran educators in the group gained a fresh perspective from the novice educators, the newer teachers were able to see veterans and professors as active practitioners who held expertise but also remained as inquirers into practice. As Amanda noted:

> [O]ne eye-opener for me was seeing that people I would consider already to be professional are still developing and they are still questioning, and they have questions just like I do after so many [years], and that's really inspiring...to know that you can constantly change and reevaluate.

This comment reverses a too-common belief that if veteran teachers do not present themselves as omniscient, then colleagues and students will not respect them. Instead, as Amanda noted, seeing veteran teachers deeply involved in refining practice gave her the impetus to do so.

This scenario casts the role of educators in a completely different light, one that is subtly and complexly shaded, yet more encompassing. Educators who critically inquire do not allow their practice to stagnate, but, instead, their practice grows, changes, questions, and adapts. As both Jennifer Aaron and Ellen Elrick note, "We encourage our students to read more to be better readers and to write more to be better writers, but as teachers, we are not encouraged to do the same thing, to learn to be better." This point returns to a point we made in chapter 2, in which educators in too many educational settings are neither given credit nor time to reflect on what is occurring in their classrooms. Instead, administrators expect teachers to complete the current topic, unit, or course in order to get to the next prescribed one as quickly as possible. We want to indicate particularly that teacher educators at universities operate under the same constraints as K–12 teachers: A typical semester length is hardly conducive to the creation of learning communities.

The problem with the conception of teaching emanating from too many legislative and governing bodies is that they don't allow for educators to be completely rounded professionals who solve problems, assess students' abilities, create learning experiences, reflect on their practices, ask questions, and engage in the art of teaching as an ongoing process. In contrast to these policies, our inquiry cohorts made time and space to encourage us to learn better as teachers and develop beyond the limited teaching identities modeled in our schools. We offered ourselves a way to get beyond these restrictive conceptions while providing a means for novice and veteran educators across the K–12/university spectrum to work together by developing a community in which taking risks and responsibility are the norm.

Transacting as Colleagues

In addition to serving as a unique professional development opportunity for teachers, we also forged a powerful partnership between teacher educators and practicing teachers. One of the criticisms we often hear leveled against teacher educators is that they are spatially and temporally removed from the inner workings of the public schools in which they research and for which they educate teachers to teach. Given that our study involved K–12 teachers and teacher educators, the teacher educators were able to interact with practicing teachers to understand how they made professional decisions as they engaged in inquiry.

It's not that those of us at the university denied our expertise. As is evident throughout chapter 3, moreover, it was important for us with experience conducting research to model that work and share with classroom teachers the "doing" of primary research. What made our community critically different, however, was that the teacher educators aimed the figurative microscope at their own practices by researching their own teaching practices. For all intents and purposes, we substantially flattened and reduced the typical hierarchy, the interloper tension that researchers sometimes encounter in the public schools, and many critical conversations across K–12 and university classrooms flourished. This structure met our individual professional needs, so we did not ignore what made us different as professionals, and we brought to the fore what made us similar as learners. Amanda captured this idea by stating:

> [We are] going beyond just our classrooms, going beyond where our goals are. I think [the work] wasn't prescribed…we all kind of came [into the proj-

ect] with our own identities and what can we do with this...we didn't know what our end goal was necessarily when we started.

Involving Observation in the Third Person

Another characteristic of our structure that was invaluable to us was the use of a third-person observer. Kathy Roulston's role as an invited outsider, someone who entered into our project at various times to provide snap-shots and sketches of the terrain of critical inquiry research, was essential to our progress. The notes and analysis she completed gave us, individually and collectively, another perspective on our work, and her "tourist" perspective allowed us to reflect more fully on our roles as teachers and researchers. We needed someone to force the group to look at its interactions within the small cohorts and across the large cohort. Eurydice commented:

> [Kathy] has moved us a great deal in looking at [ourselves]...there's some-thing fresh that comes out of that lens...that helps me to really question, "Is this where I want to go?" Some in the cohort wondered, "Would we have reflected so much on how we fit together as a group had we not had some-one asking us those specific questions?"

In addition, her work provided a sense of continuity. Specifically, her analysis allowed new members of the community to catch up quickly be-cause the documents she created fully captured the work we completed pre-viously. As Jennifer explained,

> Had I not had [Kathy's] report, I would have just really felt very lost. It grounded everything that [the large cohort] had done and positioned me where I needed to be to understand where I was jumping in. You could not have caught me up on a conversation about what everybody is doing, you know, where everybody came in. I would not have known how I fit in easily without having read [her] report.

Because inquiry can be a fairly circuitous process, Kathy's feedback served as a mapping of where we had been, a mapping that was vital as we underwent this long-term, in-depth process of collecting and analyzing data.

Furthermore, just as Bob's students and Hope Vaughn's students needed a time of reflection to make sense of their inquiry experiences, Kathy's role as an outside observer gave us the kind of written and verbal feedback that helped us to clarify what we were accomplishing as individuals, small co-horts, and a large cohort. Her insights helped bring to our attention what was plainly visible, but which we could not see.

Making an Investment in Critical Inquiry

Just as Kathy's role was vital in providing us with a third-person perspective to help us in the reflective process, the amount of time we had to sustain our inquiry was pivotal to this project. In contrast to traditional teacher professional development that lasts one or two days and just scratches the surface of any given topic, our sustained three-year project gave us the opportunity to read common texts, learn common research procedures, cross-analyze data, create texts, and present at national conferences.

Although sustained time was important to the organization of this project, the way we spent our time was critically important. Professional development was not something that was just happening to us. No, each of us actively participated as teachers and researchers. We took ownership of our professional development because we saw the need for such a project. Whereas school communities infrequently nurture teachers as intellectuals, the educators across all three cohorts nurtured one another as such. We all took the stance that, as professionals, we were still learning and developing, regardless if we were novices or veteran educators.

Andrea Pintaone-Hernandez described professional development in the large cohort in this way:

> This framework for professional development asks me for my reflection or my analysis. [My previous professional development opportunities were] often delivered to us, "the professionals," as something to change or add to our classrooms, and so it did not consider the professional in professional development.

Bob and Bren Daniell both noted, "We are not saying, 'Here is a hoop, jump through it.'" Nor were we offering professional development and presenting it as "teacher training days." Instead, as Michelle Commeyras observed, "We have talk that is sustained over time."

■ What Did We Learn About Critical Inquiry?

As we reflected on our group and individual efforts to understand critical inquiry, we concluded that all inquiry is grounded in a series of experiences that continually result in an understanding that is always in flux. We also found that our shifting definitions of inquiry resulted in a shifting of roles. Across our various classrooms, we learned that tension was ever present and played a key role in maintaining learning. However, for each of these processes to occur, it was necessary to establish community, engage in risk taking, and respond responsibly to the learning context. Subsequently, we will address what we came to understand about these processes through the lenses of establishing community, taking responsibility, and encountering risk.

Acknowledging and Accessing Layers of Critical Inquiry

Often, educators present inquiry as *the* final destination. That is, students and teachers inquire into a particular phenomenon, and, once they learn enough factual information, the need to inquire comes to an end. For many of us, the most vital aspect of critical inquiry was the continuous nature of it, the sense that we were involved in an ongoing process. Perhaps Hope said it best when she remarked:

> The most important thing I learned about critical inquiry is that it is about the process more than the final product. It, for me, is a stance one takes to investigate ideas, behavior, information, reactions, and so on. Ultimately, the end result becomes almost inconsequential because it is those things that come out during the inquiring that become the most revealing. If you end up with something great at the end of your particular study, then it is just the icing on the cake. However, I'm not sure that with critical inquiry there is an end. One question or comment leads to another. It simply leads to more learning. How exciting! That is probably the most difficult concept for me— that at the "end" of my inquiry, I may have nothing more concrete than an entirely new question.

We found that students of K–12 teachers and teacher educators needed to have numerous and sustainable opportunities to investigate their own learning of content. As Dewey (1916) noted, students must have enough learning opportunities available for fruitful experiences to take place. Of course, all classrooms provide experiences for learning, but Dewey (1938) argued that the quality of those experiences markedly ranged. From our perspective, there is a vast difference in the quality of experience when some students merely retell the facts of a story and others interrogate that story for how it relates to their lives and what meaning it might hold for them and others. The former, we feel, is a kind of education that domesticates and keeps the centripetal status quo in dominance. The latter experience, instead, is liberating in that it helps students find their own voices and the agency to use them.

Again, we are not arguing for the individual over the group, but, instead, we are proposing new relationships and ongoing negotiations between individuals and the communities they inhabit. As we mentioned in chapter 2, Bakhtin argues that all verbal transactions are social and that language and meaning are always in flux. In classrooms, teachers attempt to preserve the constructive nature of meaning while acknowledging the need for a common critical base of the content to be learned. Bob's classroom experience with Hayley and other content area students, described in detail in chapter 4, provided us with a good example of this tension. What this example poignantly shows is that there is a clear need in critical inquiry classrooms for calling learning to the surface, even to state directly and show students what they have been learning about a particular content. This is especially true in classrooms where students are not convinced that learning that matters to them is taking place. Yet, in order to help students see that critical inquiry pedagogy is working and they are learning, a critical base is necessary, and that base is ever shifting. In other words, the students needed to be engaged in critical inquiry pedagogy long enough for them to be able to pull the central points, or themes, from their investigation.

Yet one cannot say unequivocally that students are better able to reexamine what they have learned at week 5 of a semester than if they did so at week 4 or 11 of that same semester. Nor can a week be designated as *the* week to revisit the course content, regardless of the content being taught and the students' needs. Instead, what we can say is that critical inquiry classrooms do allow students to voice their discontent, as well as provide them with the space to better interrogate their beliefs. An important part of students' investigations in the classroom should include opportunities to revisit what they have learned, consider the importance and relevance of that information, and unpack the process. In doing so, teachers and students acknowledge that inquiry is occurring on many levels, and that the quality and depth of the experience better prepares them for dealing with the complexity of their future literate lives.

Shifting Roles of K–12 Teachers and Teacher Educators

Another important process that we saw as key for enacting critical inquiry pedagogy was the need for the shifting of roles. It is impossible to discuss roles in the classroom without addressing power relations in the classroom. Throughout this book, we have taken the position that educators, despite their need at times to state otherwise, cannot deny that they hold relative positions of power. After all, one can only share power if one has power to share. However, this does not preclude educators from creating learning structures that allow all participants the opportunity to question their learning or move the learning agenda in different directions. What is required is the willingness of all involved to monitor discussions and take responsibility for the learning that is occurring.

As we looked at our data, we found that the role of knowledge sharer, a key player in the learning process, shifted according to the task at hand. For example, in chapter 3, Amanda, Elizabeth, Eurydice, and Ellen highlighted Eurydice's ambivalence with knowing when to help, how much to help, and when to step back from the small-cohort interactions. What that example points out is the idea that members of a critical inquiry community should not be wedded to or precluded from a particular role in the group. The learning community should allow for individuals' strengths to play a key role. In contrast to the typical classroom discourse, there should not be one person who is always in dominance over, more knowledgeable than, or better positioned to have his or her decisions override all the others.

We all struggled with stepping outside the typical roles we had embraced. This was true whether the cohort member was a university person, who often is in charge of overseeing or conducting research, or the classroom teacher, who often is the target of the investigation and not an equal member of the research team. Moreover, this also meant that those who perhaps were too used to taking control needed, at times, to let others take those roles and to trust that what needed to get done would get done, and done well, even if it was done differently. On the other hand, those who perhaps had grown too comfortable merging into the background needed to fend off their discomfort with the limelight and allow their expertise to come to center stage. Ultimately, what our three years of collaboration revealed is that K–12 teachers and teacher educators are capable of getting outside of the typical roles society ascribes to them. However, because these practices are entrenched in us, a real desire and support must exist for a different type of interaction.

Maintaining Tension Without Overwhelming Teachers and Students

Many of us also struggled with maintaining a healthy level of tension in our classrooms while encouraging students to believe in the critical inquiry process. Throughout this book, we have presented the ways that tension existed in our inquiry community as well as in the classrooms. Lindfors (1999) argues that the ideal place for inquiry to occur is at Vygotsky's (1934/1978) Zone of Proximal Development (ZPD). Vygotsky defines ZPD as the space where learners are able to accomplish a task with a more experienced person than they would not be able to accomplish on their own. In this learning space, there is tension, but the tension is not such that one feels overwhelmed.

In many ways, we nurtured an environment that allowed various participants to operate within their ZPD with a clear understanding that they would not fall through the cracks. Jill Hermann-Wilmarth stated it best when she reflected on what she learned about critical inquiry:

> What has been important for me is to realize that, if we don't find a place for all members of a critically inquiring community to philosophically and theoretically meet, the pedagogy falls flat. Part of the process, I learned, is for students and teachers to inquire into where and why they each come to the inquiry—what stances make us each comfortable, to whom do we find ourselves accountable and why—and how to learn how to use the inquiry to challenge, confirm, or push those places of comfort. To me, success as a critically inquiring educator means that my students and I leave the semester or the year with further inquiries into our teaching, ourselves, and our learning.

Key to Jill's example is that she did not throw her students into unknown territory, which, in this case, is critical inquiry. Instead, she purposely and figuratively walked toward them and met them at the center, where she asked and expected them to engage in critical inquiry with her.

Another important component to critical inquiry pedagogy that educators often overlook is the need to engage in metacognition as part of the inquiry process. Metacognition in many ways can alleviate some of the tension often associated with participating in inquiry. The tension is a result of how risky critical inquiry is to embrace in today's teaching climate as well as our inexperience with such a pedagogy. We see critical inquiry as a means for encouraging metacognitive thinking to occur, which provides teachers and students a place where clarity is evident. For example, Kathy's reports provided a third-person perspective on our collective work that gave all of us a place to begin our metacognition on what we had been learning from our inquiry. Likewise, Bob's student, Hayley, provided the moment for metacognition in his class when she asked the question, "What is content area reading?" Both examples provided opportunities to brainstorm and reflect on what had been accomplished and created a safer feeling about the next step to be taken in the classroom.

Integrating Community, Responsibility, and Risk
In writing this book, we have, to an extent, taken our critical inquiry community apart and examined each of the pieces, perhaps in juxtaposition, but

still somewhat individually. It's time to put the components back together. Although the Champaign, Illinois, USA, cohort focused on community and the two Athens, Georgia, USA, cohorts focused on responsibility and risk taking, respectively, in actuality we all were simultaneously focusing on all three areas, even if we gave the nod to one above the others. But we can conceive of no critical inquiry situation that is not dependent on the ways educators and learners build community, take responsibility, and encourage risk taking. The transaction of these three aspects of critical inquiry classrooms frequently is, and there is no other word for it, critical to what occurs there.

Therefore, although Sharon Dowling Cox was concerned about the risks she and her students were taking as they rethought how they would address communication problems in her classroom, she also was concerned with the community she was building as she took responsibility for her teaching decisions and her students took greater control of their own learning. Ellen may have been worried about the issue of community in her elementary classroom, but she also took responsibility for her own risks as she encouraged her students to become more involved in their work. Bren, wondering if she was asking too much of herself and her students as they discussed issues of race and culture, had to grapple with that responsibility and what it meant for the community inside and outside her classroom. When Zaria, Andrea's student, took responsibility for her own learning in Andrea's classroom, they both took risks that affected the learning community that was in place. As Michelle considered with her students the risk of sharing concerns that they had raised, she plotted a course that she hoped would foster a new kind of community in the classroom, one that was built upon students taking more responsibility for their own actions.

We could go on, but we think we have made the point: A critical inquiry classroom is a complex set of ongoing transactions, not the least of which concern what counts as community, what responsibility we take for that community, and what risk taking looks like inside that community. To speak of one of these concerns is to consider the others. To fail to do this and to fail to leave oneself open to other transactions is to shortchange the learning of all involved in that critical inquiry community.

■ Rich Deposit, Rich Return

As we discussed in chapter 1, making little investment in the lives of public education students and teachers will yield equally small returns. Society gets back from the system only that which it puts in. If we continue to make only inconsequential financial, emotional, and intellectual deposits into public education, then we continue to reap little in return.

This lack of sizable financial, emotional, and intellectual deposits is . widespread. We see it in the underfunding and narrow conceptions of punitive U.S. federal and state educational policy and in the general public's resistance to imagine school differently from what they experienced in earlier times. We see it in the classes of some teacher educators who, rather than helping preservice and inservice teachers develop sound philosophical stances, either feed a "bag-of-educational-tricks" mentality by stocking their methods courses full of cute, but largely limited-in-use activities or throw up their hands in despair as soon as undergraduates get uncomfortable with sociocultural and sociopolitical issues. We see it in the work of some teachers who are too easily cowed by administrative mandates and assume they have no voice to resist or enact change. We see it in the emerging practices of some preservice teachers who conceive of teaching as a job rather than an investment in our present and future lives. We see it in the apathy of some parents who see schools mostly as government-supplied caregiving facilities rather than places of intellectual stimulation and growth. We see it in the responses of some students who may comply with the system but place no value in it, and expect "no return" on their minimal investment. When all these stakeholders make "no deposit" in our community schools, we individually and collectively gain nothing "in return."

Critical inquiry and critical inquiry pedagogy require investments—of time, interest, trust, expectations, support, hope, community building, responsibility, and risk. Curiously, it requires far less money than our current system of testing, although a redirection of that money would facilitate teaching that expects teachers and students to inquire together. Why do we continue paying test publishers and professional development consultants enormous sums of money to provide tests—that are, at their best, benign but too narrow to give a true assessment of students and school achievement, and, at their worst, malevolent in their ability to marginalize and oppress those they purport to lift up? Why not invest that money in resources that would lower class size and provide technology-equipped classrooms that invite, rather than repel, students? What we would reap from these investments would be a spike in returns—of engagement, depth of learning, community, responsibility, and risk taking.

But we understand that, under the current U.S. political climate, what we ask is difficult to achieve. As our project developed, the educators within all three small cohorts experienced varying degrees of outside pressure from U.S.

district, state, and national mandates. By this project's end, we felt pressure from testing mandates and a narrowing curriculum to focus on test preparation. Although inquiry often seems too risky to engage in while such an overwhelming emphasis on text preparation pervades, none of us wanted to abdicate our dedication to rich teaching and learning within the context of preparing students for testing. Plus, if we really were to actualize our beliefs, then we needed to put our praxis where our minds were.

As a result, those of us remaining in the classroom at this project's end spent enormous amounts of time juggling vital, rich teaching with test preparation, trying to at least provide a level of inquiry to the latter. This intersection of centripetal and centrifugal forces created new questions such as, "Where do testing and inquiry meet? What is the effect of standardized testing on critical inquiry pedagogy? What is the impact of critical inquiry pedagogy on standardized testing?"

Our work shows that with "no deposit," there will be "no return." Stakeholders need to work in communities where we are encouraged to take responsibility for the learning in U.S. classrooms and where we empower students to claim a stake in their own learning. This achievement will require all of us to take enormous risks, because, unlike the factory where bottles are uniformly manufactured and filled with identical liquids, we in education are dealing with human beings—physical, intellectual, and spiritual beings of infinite variety. We need classrooms that respond to that diversity and complexity in ways that include that diversity and complexity rather than expecting a conformity to one set of values, expectations, and performances.

Can critical inquiry pedagogy offer hope for public education? Is there a place within the current educational climate for Giussani's (2001) sense of what it means to take a critical stance on understanding the world as an "invitation to try to understand what one is faced with, to discover a new good, a new truth, to extract a more mature and deeper sense of satisfaction" (p. 10)? As Bob often reminded us, critical inquiry is a framework rather than a model: It allows teachers to be adaptable and to suit their instruction to their contexts. Rather than being antithetical to standardized curriculums and testing, critical inquiry is a pedagogy that can help teachers to open up even the most restrictive curriculum. By asking teachers and students to inquire into, as Freire (1970/1993) notes, the word and the world, we create a means in which the making of meaning takes precedence over rote response, whether that classroom is composed of first-grade students or university seniors.

Project Participants Organized by Cohort

	Participants	Teaching Position[1]	Institution
Risk-Taking Cohort, Athens, Georgia, USA	Bren Daniell	Fifth-grade teacher	Honey Creek Elementary School, Conyers, Georgia, USA
	Sharon Dowling Cox[2]	Speech–language pathologist	Honey Creek Elementary School, Conyers, Georgia, USA
	Jill Hermann-Wilmarth	Teacher educator	Language Education, University of Georgia, Athens, Georgia, USA
	Michelle Commeyras	Teacher educator	Reading Education, University of Georgia, Athens, Georgia, USA
Responsibility Cohort, Athens, Georgia, USA	Bob Fecho	Teacher educator	Reading Education, University of Georgia, Athens, Georgia, USA
	Hope Vaughn	Sixth-grade language arts teacher	Elbert County Middle School, Elberton, Georgia, USA
	Andrea Pintaone-Hernandez	Second-grade teacher[3,4]	South Jackson School, Athens, Georgia, USA
		Head Start teacher[5]	Oconee County Head Start, Bogart, Georgia, USA
	Jennifer Aaron[2]	Reading specialist	Chase Elementary School, Athens, Georgia, USA
Community Cohort, Champaign, Illinois, USA	Elizabeth Hogan[2]	High school English teacher	Centennial High School, Champaign, Illinois, USA
	Amanda Siegel	Third-,[5] fourth-,[3] and fifth-grade teacher[3,6]	Dr. Howard Elementary School, Champaign, Illinois, USA
		Third-grade teacher	Dr. Howard Elementary School, Champaign, Illinois, USA
	Eurydice Bouchereau Bauer	Teacher educator	Education, The University of Illinois, Champaign, Illinois, USA
	Ellen Elrick	Second-grade teacher	Dr. Howard Elementary School, Champaign, Illinois, USA

[1] Teaching positions and affiliations were at the time of the project.
[2] New cohort member for 2002–2003.
[3] First year of cohort participation.
[4] Between years one and two of participation in the work of our cohorts, Andrea left South Jackson School for a position as a Head Start teacher in another county.
[5] Second year of cohort participation.
[6] Between years one and two of participation in the work of our cohorts, Amanda remained at the same school but received a new grade assignment.

Individual and Small-Cohort Research Topics and Data Inventory

Cohort Focus	Participants	Research Topic	Data Collection	Analysis
Developing Community	Elizabeth Hogan	What are the outcomes for students' learning from participation in Socratic seminars in a high school classroom?	Teacher reflections, student work samples, transcriptions of videotapes of classes, student interviews, student surveys, lesson plans, demographic data	Examination of students' views, transcripts of classroom interaction, and student work samples
	Amanda Siegel	How might a community for dialogue between third-, fourth-, and fifth-grade students be built around literature discussions?	Teacher reflections, students' reading and writing surveys, read-alouds on chart paper, audiotapes of small- and large-group discussions	Examination of questioning in classroom interaction
	Eurydice Bouchereau Bauer	What does classroom interaction look like in my undergraduate classroom? How might teacher educators support teachers investigating their own inquiries in classrooms?	Weekly teacher reflections, student journals, focus-group interviews with students, transcripts of small-group interactions, videotapes and audiotapes of classroom discussions	Examination of the links between a teacher's aims and students' needs

(continued)

Cohort Focus	Participants	Research Topic	Data Collection	Analysis
Developing Community	Ellen Elrick	How do students in a second-grade class develop as writers? What is the journey of their teacher?	Teacher journals and reflections, student work samples, student surveys, videotapes of classroom literacy lessons, transcripts of classroom conversations	Examination of the teacher's journey and students' journeys as writers
Taking Responsibility	Bob Fecho	How does inquiry work in an undergraduate classroom?	Weekly teacher journal, mathematics majors' weekly e-mail reactions to class activities, student work samples, student interviews, field notes of observations by other observers	Examination of when or how students took responsibility for asking their own questions
	Hope Vaughn	What happens in contact zones where administrators', students', and teachers' agendas transact?	Teacher journal, student work samples	Reading and rereading data set, focusing on identification of sections of data set relevant to the theme of "taking responsibility"
	Andrea Pintaone-Hernandez	How do students and a teacher in a second-grade classroom take ownership and responsibility for their learning?	Teacher journal, field notes from observations by small-cohort members, student work samples	Use of the descriptive review process
	Jennifer Aaron	How does critical inquiry play out in a fifth-grade classroom undertaking a service-learning project?	Student writing samples, student reflections, teacher journals, interviews with fifth-grade students, audio-recorded classroom discussions, field notes of observations by other observers	Examination of where students take responsibility for their learning *(continued)*

Cohort Focus	Participants	Research Topic	Data Collection	Analysis
Taking Risks	Bren Daniell	How might fifth-grade students' tolerance for diversity and sense of social consciousness be developed?	Transcripts of audiotaped book discussions, teacher journals, student journals, student work samples, lesson plans, comments from cohort group concerning data	Examination of student and teacher responses to readings
	Sharon Dowling Cox	What kinds of strategies might fifth-grade students use to improve their communication skills?	Transcriptions of audio recordings of class sessions, students' reflections, teacher journals, student interviews	Identification of changes across the school year, examination of students' analysis of their audio-recorded communication
	Jill Hermann-Wilmarth	What are the experiences of an out-lesbian teacher and her preservice teacher students as they examine a variety of "risky topics"? How might teachers approach risky topics with their students?	Students' evaluations of their teacher, student interviews, classroom conversations	Examination of students' language in evaluations of their teacher
	Michelle Commeyras	How can critical inquiry pedagogy be incorporated in a reading methods course for preservice teachers?	Student work samples, transcripts from small-cohort meetings, students' e-mail postings	Descriptive review process, poetic analysis, multiple perspectives

REFERENCES

Adams, K., & Emery, K. (1994). Classroom coming out stories: Practical strategies for productive self-disclosure. In L. Garber (Ed.), *Tilting the tower: Lesbians teaching queer subjects* (pp. 25–34). New York: Routledge.

Allen, J. (Ed.). (1999). *Class actions: Teaching for social justice in elementary and middle school*. New York: Teachers College Press.

American Speech-Language-Hearing Association. (2001). *Roles and responsibilities with respect to reading and writing in children and adolescents* (Technical Report 21). Rockville, MD: Author.

Bakhtin, M.M. (1981). Discourse in the novel. In M. Holquist (Ed.), *The dialogic imagination: Four essays by M.M. Bakhtin* (C. Emerson & M. Holquist, Trans.; pp. 259–422). Austin: University of Texas Press.

Bakhtin, M.M. (1986). *Speech genres and other late essays* (C. Emerson & M. Holquist, Eds.; V. McGee, Trans.). Austin: University of Texas Press.

Baldwin, J. (1988). A talk to teachers. In R. Simonson & S. Walker (Eds.), *The graywolf annual five: Multicultural literacy: Opening the American mind* (pp. 3–12). St. Paul, MN: Graywolf Press.

Ballenger, C. (1999). *Teaching other people's children: Literacy and learning in a bilingual classroom*. New York: Teachers College Press

Baumann, J., Bisplinghoff, B., & Allen, J. (1997). Methodology in teacher research: Three cases. In J. Flood, S.B. Heath, & D. Lapp (Eds.), *Handbook of research on teaching literacy through the communicative and visual arts* (pp. 121–143). New York: Macmillan.

Bradbury, H., & Reason, P. (2001). Conclusion: Broadening the bandwidth of validity: Issues and choice-points for improving the quality of action research. In P. Reason & H. Bradbury (Eds.), *Handbook of action research: Participative inquiry and practice* (pp. 447–455). Thousand Oaks, CA: Sage.

Brown v. Board of Educ., 347 U.S. 483 (1954).

Burnaford, G.E., Fischer, J., & Hobson, D. (2001). *Teachers doing research: The power of action through inquiry* (2nd ed.). Mahwah, NJ: Erlbaum.

Carini, P.F. (2001). *Starting strong: A different look at children, schools, and standards*. New York: Teachers College Press.

Cazden, C.B. (1988). *Classroom discourse: The language of teaching and learning*. Portsmouth, NH: Heinemann.

Cervetti, G., Pardales, M.J., & Damico, J.S. (2001). A tale of differences: Comparing the traditions, perspectives, and educational goals of critical reading and critical literacy. *Reading Online*. Retrieved July 19, 2005, from http://www.readingonline.org/articles/art_index.asp?HREF=/articles/cervetti

Clark, C.M. (Ed.). (2001). *Talking shop: Authentic conversation and teacher learning*. New York: Teachers College Press.

Cochran-Smith, M., & Lytle, S.L. (1993). *Inside/outside: Teacher research and knowledge*. New York: Teachers College Press.

Cochran-Smith, M., & Lytle, S.L. (1999). Relationships of knowledge and practice: Teacher learning in communities. In A. Iran-Nejad & P.D. Pearson (Eds.), *Review of research in education* (Vol. 24). Washington, DC: American Educational Research Association.

Commeyras, M. (1993). Promoting critical thinking through dialogical-thinking reading lessons. *The Reading Teacher, 46*(6), 486–494.

Commeyras, M., & Kelly, K. (2002). A "found" poem from a reading odyssey. *Journal of Adolescent & Adult Literacy, 46*(2), 100–102.

Commeyras, M., & Sumner, G. (1998). Literature questions children want to discuss: What teachers and students learned in a second-grade classroom. *The Elementary School Journal, 99*(2), 129–152.

Daines, J., Daines, C., & Graham, B. (1993). *Adult reading, adult learning* (3rd ed.). Nottingham, England: Department of Adult Education, University of Nottingham.

Delpit, L.D. (1995). *Other people's children: Cultural conflict in the classroom.* New York: New Press.

Dewey, J. (1916). *Democracy and education: An introduction to the philosophy of education.* New York: Macmillan.

Dewey, J. (1938). *Experience and education.* New York: Macmillan.

Dewey, J., & Bentley, A. (1949). *Knowing and the known.* Boston: Beacon Press.

Edmondson, J. (2004). *Understanding and applying critical policy study: Reading educators advocating for change.* Newark, DE: International Reading Association.

Ellis, C., & Bochner, A.P. (2000). Autoethnography, personal narrative, reflexivity: Researcher as subject. In N.K. Denzin & Y.S. Lincoln (Eds.), *Handbook of qualitative research* (2nd ed., pp. 733–768). Thousand Oaks, CA: Sage.

Emerson, C., & Holquist, M. (1981). Glossary. In M. Holquist (Ed.), *The dialogic imagination: Four essays by M.M. Bakhtin* (C. Emerson & M. Holquist, Trans.; pp. 423–434). Austin: University of Texas Press.

Fecho, B. (2004). *"Is this English?" Race, language, and culture in the classroom.* New York: Teachers College Press.

Fecho, B., & Allen, J. (2002). Teachers researching communities of practice for social justice. *School Field, 12*(3–4), 119–141.

Fecho, B., & Allen, J. (2003). Teacher inquiry into literacy, social justice, and power. In J. Flood, D. Lapp, J.R. Squire, & J.M. Jensen (Eds.), *Handbook of research on teaching the English language arts* (2nd ed., pp. 232–246). Mahwah, NJ: Erlbaum.

Fecho, B., Allen, J., Mazaros, C., & Inyega, H. (2006). Contemplating the complexities: Teacher research on composition. In P. Smagorinsky (Ed.), *Research on composition: Multiple perspectives on two decades of change* (pp. 108–140). New York: Teachers College Press and the National Conference on Research in Language and Literacy.

Fecho, B., Commeyras, M., Bauer, E.B., & Font, G. (2000). In rehearsal: Complicating authority in undergraduate critical-inquiry classrooms. *Journal of Literacy Research, 32*(4), 471–504.

Foucault, M. (1995). *Discipline and punish: The birth of the prison* (2nd ed., A. Sheridan, Trans.). New York: Vintage. (Original work published 1977)

Franklin, E. (Ed.). (1999). *Reading and writing in more than one language: Lessons for teachers.* Alexandria, VA: Teachers of English to Speakers of Other Languages.

Freire, P. (1983). The importance of the act of reading. *Journal of Education, 165*(1), 5–11.

Freire, P. (1993). *Pedagogy of the oppressed* (M.B. Ramos, Trans.). New York: Continuum. (Original work published 1970)

Freire, P. (1998). *Teachers as cultural workers: Letters to those who dare to teach* (D. Macedo, D. Koike, & A. Oliveira, Trans.). Boulder, CO: Westview Press.

Freire, P., & Macedo, D.P. (1987). *Literacy: Reading the word and the world.* Westport, CT: Bergin & Garvey.

Freire, P., & Macedo, D.P. (1996). A dialogue: Culture, language, and race. In P. Leistyna, A. Woodrum, & S. Sherblom (Eds.), *Breaking free: The transformative power of critical pedagogy* (pp. 199–228). Cambridge, MA: Harvard Educational Review.

Gallas, K. (2003). *Imagination and literacy: A teacher's search for the heart of learning.* New York: Teachers College Press.

Garber, L. (Ed.). (1994). *Tilting the tower: Lesbians teaching queer subjects.* New York: Routledge.

Giussani, L. (2001). *The risk of education: Discovering our ultimate destiny* (R.M. Giammanco Frongia, Trans.). New York: Crossroad.

Graham, P., Hudson-Ross, S., Adkins, C., McWhorter, P., & Stewart, J. (1999). *Teacher/mentor: A dialogue for collaborative learning.* New York: Teachers College Press.

Gustavsen, B. (2001). Theory and practice: The mediating discourse. In P. Reason & H. Bradbury (Eds.), *Handbook of action research: Participant inquiry and practice* (pp. 17–26). Thousand Oaks, CA: Sage.

Hade, D.D. (1997). Reading multiculturally. In V.J. Harris (Ed.), *Using multiethnic literature in the K–8 classroom* (pp. 233–240). Norwood, MA: Christopher-Gordon.

Hankins, K.H. (2003). *Teaching through the storm: A journal of hope.* New York: Teachers College Press.

Hermans, H.J.M., & Kempen, H.J.G. (1993). *The dialogical self: Meaning as movement.* San Diego, CA: Academic.

Himley, M. (Ed.) (with Carini, P.F.). (2000). *From another angle: Children's strengths and school standards.* New York: Teachers College Press.

Hitchcock, M., & Ice, T. (2004). *The truth behind Left Behind.* Sisters, OR: Mutnomah Publishers.

Hollingsworth, S., & Sockett, H. (Eds.). (1994). *Teacher research and educational reform* (93rd yearbook of the National Society for the Study of Education). Chicago: National Society for the Study of Education.

Holquist, M. (1986). Introduction. In C. Emerson & M. Holquist (Eds.), *M.M. Bakhtin: Speech genres and other late essays* (V.W. McGee, Trans.). Austin: University of Texas Press. (Original work published 1979)

Holt, J.C. (1982). *How children fail* (Rev. ed.). New York: Delacorte Press/Seymour Lawrence.

hooks, b. (1994). *Teaching to transgress: Education as the practice of freedom.* New York: Routledge.

Hopkins, D. (2002). *A teacher's guide to classroom research* (3rd ed.). Buckingham, England: Open University Press.

Howey, N., & Samuels, E. (Eds.). (2000). *Out of the ordinary: Growing up with gay, lesbian, and transgender parents.* New York: St. Martin's Press.

Hubbard, R.S., & Power, B.M. (1999). *Living the questions: A guide for teacher-researchers.* York, ME: Stenhouse.

Hubbard, R.S., & Power, B.M. (2003). *The art of classroom inquiry: A handbook for teacher-researchers* (Rev. ed.). Portsmouth, NH: Heinemann.

Isaacs, W.N. (1993). Taking flight: Dialogue, collective thinking, and organizational learning. *Organizational Dynamics, 22*(2), 24–39.

Knowles, M. (1980). *The modern practice of adult education.* Chicago: Follet.

Kohn, A. (2000). *The case against standardized testing: Raising the scores, ruining the schools.* Portsmouth, NH: Heinemann.

Kosciw, J. (2004). *The 2003 National School Climate Survey: The school-related experiences of our nation's lesbian, gay, bisexual, and transgender youth.* New York: Gay, Lesbian, and Straight Education Network.

Ladson-Billings, G. (1994). *The dreamkeepers: Successful teachers of African American children.* San Francisco: Jossey-Bass.

Lankshear, C., & Knobel, M. (2003). *New literacies: Changing knowledge and classroom learning.* Buckingham, England: Open University Press; Philadelphia: Society for Research into Higher Education.

Larson, V.L., & McKinley, N. (1995). *Language disorders in older students: Preadolescents and adolescents.* Eau Claire, WI: Thinking Publications.

Leahy, M.M. (2004). Therapy talk: Analyzing therapeutic discourse. *Language, Speech, & Hearing Services in Schools, 35*(1), 70–81.

Lindfors, J.W. (1999). *Children's inquiry: Using language to make sense of the world.* New York: Teachers College Press.

Lytle, S.L. (2000). Teacher research in the contact zone. In M.L. Kamil, P.B. Mosenthal, P.D. Pearson, & R. Barr (Eds.), *Handbook of reading research* (Vol. 3, pp. 691–718). Mahwah, NJ: Erlbaum.

MacLean, M.S., & Mohr, M.M. (1999). *Teacher-researchers at work.* Berkeley: National Writing Project, University of California.

McNiff, J., Lomax, P., & Whitehead, J. (2004). *You and your action research project* (2nd ed.). New York: RoutledgeFalmer.

Mehan, H. (1978). Structuring school structure. *Harvard Educational Review, 48*(1), 32–64.

Michie, G. (1999). *Holler if you hear me: The education of a teacher and his students.* New York: Teachers College Press.

Miller, D. (2002). *Reading with meaning: Teaching comprehension in the primary grades.* Portland, ME: Stenhouse.

Miner, B. (1998). Reading, writing, and censorship: When reading good books can get schools in trouble: First of two articles. *Rethinking Schools, 12*(3), 4–7. Retrieved October 16, 2005, from http://www.rethinkingschools.org/archive/12_03/cenmain.shtml;geturl=d+highlightmatches+gotofirstmatch;terms=censorship;enc=censorship;utf8=on;noparts#firstmatch

Mittler, M.L., & Blumenthal, A. (1994). On being a change agent: Teacher as text, homophobia as context. In L. Garber (Ed.), *Tilting the tower: Lesbians teaching queer subjects* (pp. 3–10). New York: Routledge.

Mohr, M.M., Rogers, C., Sanford, B., Nocerino, M.A., MacLean, M.S., & Clawson, S. (2004). *Teacher research for better schools.* New York: Teachers College Press; Berkeley: National Writing Project, University of California.

Murphy, S. (with Shannon, P., Johnston, P., & Hansen, J.). (1998). *Fragile evidence: A critique of reading assessment.* Mahwah, NJ: Erlbaum.

National Commission on Service-Learning. (2002). *Learning in deed: The power of service-learning for American schools*. Newton, MA: Author.

National Institute of Child Health and Human Development. (2000). *Report of the · National Reading Panel. Teaching children to read: An evidence-based assessment of the scientific research literature on reading and its implications for reading instruction* (NIH Publication No. 00-4769). Washington, DC: U.S. Government Printing Office.

New London Group. (2000). A pedagogy of multiliteracies: Designing social futures. In B. Cope & M. Kalantzis (Eds.), *Multiliteracies: Literacy learning and the design of social futures*. London: Routledge.

Patton, M.Q. (2002). *Qualitative research and evaluation methods* (3rd ed.). Thousand Oaks, CA: Sage.

Peirce, C.S. (1931–1958). *Collected papers of Charles Sanders Peirce* (Vols. 1–8, C. Hartshone & P. Weiss, Eds.). Cambridge, MA: Harvard University Press.

Pintaone-Hernandez, A.M. (2002). *Literacy narratives toward identity and community in a first-grade classroom*. Unpublished master's thesis, University of Georgia, Athens.

Pratt, M.L. (1991). Arts of the contact zone. *Profession, 91*, 33–40.

Reed, V.A., & Spicer, L. (2003). The relative importance of selected communication skills for adolescents' interactions with their teachers: High school teachers' opinions. *Language, Speech, & Hearing Services in Schools, 34*(4), 343–357.

Renn, O. (1992). Concepts of risk: A classification. In S. Krimsky & D. Golding (Eds.), *Social theories of risk* (pp. 53–79). Westport, CT: Praeger.

Richards, I.A. (1950). *Practical criticism: A study of literary judgment*. New York: Harcourt, Brace. (Original work published 1929)

Rosenblatt, L.M. (1994). The transactional theory of reading and writing. In R.B. Ruddell, M.R. Ruddell, & H. Singer (Eds.), *Theoretical models and processes of reading* (4th ed., pp. 1057–1092). Newark, DE: International Reading Association.

Rosenblatt, L.M. (1995). *Literature as exploration* (5th ed.). New York: Modern Language Association. (Original work published 1938)

Schratz, M., & Walker, R. (1995). *Research as social change: New opportunities for qualitative research*. New York: Routledge.

Schultz, K., & Fecho, B. (2005). Literacies in adolescence: An analysis of policies from the United States and Queensland, Australia. In *International Handbook of Educational Policy* (pp. 677–694). The Netherlands: Kluwer Academic Publishers.

Shor, I. (1992). *Empowering education*. Chicago: University of Chicago Press.

Singer, B.D., & Bashir, A.S. (1999). What are executive functions and self-regulation and what do they have to do with language-learning disorders? *Language, Speech, & Hearing Services in Schools, 30*(3), 265–273.

Sullivan, A.M. (2005). Lessons from the Anhinga Trail: Poetry and teaching. In R. Lawrence (Ed.), *Artistic ways of knowing: Expanded opportunities for teaching and learning* (pp. 23–32). San Francisco: Jossey Bass.

Tyack, D.B., & Cuban, L. (1995). *Tinkering toward utopia: A century of public school reform*. Cambridge, MA: Harvard University Press.

Vygotsky, L.S. (1978). *Mind in society: The development of higher psychological processes* (M. Cole, V. John-Steiner, S. Scribner, & E. Souberman, Eds. & Trans.). Cambridge, MA: Harvard University Press. (Original work published 1934)

Vygotsky, L.S. (1986). *Thought and language* (A. Kozalin, Trans.). Cambridge, MA: The MIT Press. (Original work published 1934)

Webster's ninth new collegiate dictionary (ninth ed.). (1988). Springfield, MA: Merriam-Webster.

Wiggins, G.P., & McTighe, J. (1998). *Understanding by design*. Alexandria, VA: Association for Supervision and Curriculum Development.

Wilhelm, J.D. (1997). *"You gotta be the book": Teaching engaged and reflective reading with adolescents*. New York: Teachers College Press.

Zeichner, K.M. (1993). *Action research: Personal renewal and social reconstruction*. Educational Action Research, *1*(2), 199–219.

LITERATURE CITED

Adler, D.A. (1989). *A picture book of Martin Luther King, Jr.* Ill. R. Casilla. New York: Holiday House.

Bierce, A. (2004). An occurrence at Owl Creek Bridge. In E.V. Roberts & H.E. Jacobs (Eds.), *Literature: An introduction to reading and writing* (7th ed., pp. 226–232). Upper Saddle River, NJ: Pearson Prentice Hall. (Original work published 1891)

Blainey, G. (1982). *The tyranny of distance: How distance shaped Australia's history* (Rev. ed.). Sydney, NSW, Australia: Pan Macmillan.

Bunting, E. (1988). *How many days to America? A Thanksgiving story*. Ill. B. Peck. New York: Clarion Books.

Esquivel, L. (1992). *Like water for chocolate: A novel in monthly installments, with recipes, romances, and home remedies* (C. Christensen & T. Christensen, Trans.). New York: Doubleday.

Garden, N. (2000). *Holly's secret*. New York: Farrar Straus Giroux.

Hoffman, M. (1991). *Amazing Grace*. Ill. C. Binch. New York: Dial Books for Young Readers.

Holm, J.L. (2001). *Our only May Amelia*. New York: HarperTrophy.

Jackson, S. (2004). The lottery. In E.V. Roberts & H.E. Jacobs (Ed.), *Literature: An introduction to reading and writing* (5th ed.; pp. 233–241). Upper Saddle River, NJ: Pearson Prentice Hall. (Original work published 1948)

Mushonga, A. (2001). *Kapitau and the magic whistle*. Harare, Zimbabwe: Priority Projects Publishing.

Naylor, P.R. (2000). *Shiloh*. New York: Aladdin.

Ringgold, F. (1991). *Tar beach*. New York: Crown.

Ringgold, F. (1992). *Aunt Harriet's underground railroad in the sky*. New York: Crown.

Salinger, J.D. (1963). *Raise high the roof beam, carpenters*. Boston: Little, Brown. (Original work published 1959)

Shakespeare, W. (2004). *Hamlet, Prince of Denmark*. In E.V. Roberts & H.E. Jacobs (Eds.), *Literature: An introduction to reading and writing* (Vol. 7, pp. 1245–1345). Upper Saddle River, NJ: Pearson Prentice Hall.

Smith, R. (1989). *Chocolate fever*. Ill. G. Fiammenghi. New York: Putnam. (Original work published 1972)

Sophocles. (2004). Oedipus the king. In E.V. Roberts & H.E. Jacobs (Eds.), *Literature: An introduction to reading and writing* (5th ed., pp. 1197–1236). Upper Saddle River, NJ: Pearson Prentice Hall.

Soto, G. (1995). *Chato's kitchen*. Ill. S. Guevara. New York: Putnam.

Taylor, M.D. (1976). *Roll of thunder, hear my cry*. New York: Dial Press.

Taylor, M.D. (1998). *The friendship*. Ill. M. Ginsburg. New York: Penguin Putnam Books for Young Readers.

Thomas, D. (2004). Do not go gently into that good night. In E.V. Roberts & H.E. Jacobs (Eds.), *Literature: An introduction to reading and writing* (5th ed., p. 842). Upper Saddle River, NJ: Pearson Prentice Hall. (Original work published 1952)

Williams, T. (1945). *The glass menagerie: A play*. New York: Random House.

MOTION PICTURES AND AUDIO RECORDING CITED

Brooks, J., Crowe, C., Mark, L., & Sakai, R. (Producers) & Crowe, C. (Director). (1996). *Jerry Maguire* [Motion picture]. United States: Tristar Pictures.

Cosby, B. (Monologist). (1998). *I started out as a child*. (Compact Disc Recording #1567). Los Angeles: Warner Brothers.

Katzka, G., & Scherick, E.J. (Producers), Sargent, J. (Director), & Stone, P. (Writer). (1974). *The taking of Pelham one two three* [Motion picture]. United States: United Artists Corporation.

Levin, M. (Producer/Writer/Director), Stratton, R. (Writer/Producer), Williams, S. (Writer), Sohn, S. (Writer), & Kessler, H.M. (Producer). (1998). *Slam* [Motion picture]. United States: Trimark.

McArthur, S., Schumaker, T. (Producers), Allers, R., & Minkoff, R. (Directors). (2003). *The lion king* [Motion picture]. United States: Disney.

Palcy, E. (Producer/Director). (1998). *Ruby Bridges* [Motion picture]. United States: Disney.

Selznick, D.O. (Producer), Howard, S. (Writer), & Fleming, V. (Director). (1939). *Gone with the wind* [Motion picture]. United States: Metro-Goldwyn Mayer.

INDEX

Note: Page numbers followed by *t* indicate tables.

A

B

C

HOWARD, S., 99
HOWEY, N., 94
HUBBARD, R.S., 143
HUDSON-ROSS, S., 15

I

ICE, T., 116
INDIVIDUALISM: importance of, 21–23
INQUIRY: in content areas, 68–74; versus critical inquiry, 3; definition of, 13; participative, 144; relevance of, 6–70
INQUIRY COMMUNITY: concept of, 23–24
INTERNALLY PERSUASIVE DISCOURSE, 55, 59
INTERVIEWS: students and, 84
INYEGA, H., 15
ISAACS, W.N., 38

J

JACKSON, S., 46
JOHNSTON, P., 66

K

KATZKA, G., 89
KELLY, K., 117
KEMPEN, H.J.G., 29
KESSLER, H.M., 114
KNOBEL, M., 96
KNOWLES, M., 151
KOHN, A., 66
KOSCIW, J., 94
K–12 TEACHERS: relations with teacher educators, 7–8, 17, 126, 132–133, 149–150; roles of, shifting, 156–157; on taking responsibility, 135; and theory, 21–22

L

LADSON-BILLINGS, G., 50
LAHAYE, TIM, 116
LANGUAGE: assumptions about, 114–118
LANKSHEAR, C., 96
LARGE COHORT, 7; responsibility to, significance of, 139–140; sharing responsibility among, 133–137; ways of working in, 121–145. *See also* research community
LARSON, V.L., 92–93, 104
LEAHY, M.M., 106
LEVIN, M., 114
LINDFORS, J.W., 13, 35, 47, 53, 55, 157
LOG: reflective, 51
LOMAX, P., 143
LYLE SPENCER FOUNDATION, 6
LYTLE, S.L., 15, 143

M

Macedo, D.P., 27, 57
MacLean, M.S., 15, 143
Mark, L., 21
Mazaros, C., 15
McArthur, S., 112
McKinley, N., 92–93, 104
McNiff, J., 143
McTighe, J., 88
McWhorter, P., 15
Mehan, H., 44
Michie, G., 15
Miller, D., 52
Miner, B., 110
Minkoff, R., 112
Mittler, M.L., 109
modeling: in Socratic seminar, 45
Mohr, M.M., 15, 143
multicultural reading, 112–113
Murphy, S., 66
Mushonga, A., 100

N

National Commission on Service-Learning, 86
National Institute of Child Health and Human Development, 95
Naylor, P.R., 98, 100
networks: and school reform, 144
New London Group, 25, 66
Nocerino, M.A., 15
novice teachers: on teacher research project, 138–139

O

observation. See external evaluator
ownership: academic service learning and, 82–87; and English classroom, 74–78; students and teachers and, 67–68

P

Palcy, E., 97
Pardales, M.J., 95
participative inquiry, 144
Patton, M.Q., 124
Pierce, C.S., 24
Pintaone-Hernandez, A.M., 29, 148
policymakers: versus authentic interaction, 58–59; and classroom agenda, 65–66, 90
Power, B.M., 143
practitioner research. See teacher research
Pratt, M.L., 27
praxis, 26–28; definition of, 109

PRESERVICE TEACHERS: assumptions about language, 114–118; self-interrogation by, 109–114

PRISONERS: and language, 115–118

PRIVILEGE: self-interrogation of, 112–113

Q

QUESTIONS: authentic, 54–55; and authentic discussion, 47–48; of community cohort, 34–36; organizing class around, 44–47; raising, 1–18; of responsibility cohort, 62–64; of risk cohort, 92–95; student generated, 48–49, 51, 54–55; teacher generated, 50–51

R

READING: in content areas, 68–74; social context of, 112

REASON, P., 144–145

REED, V.A., 92

REFLECTION: egocentrism and, 4; in research framework, 150–152; time for, 88–89, 140–141

REFLECTIVE LOG, 51

RENN, O., 96

REQUEST-RESPONSE-EVALUATION (RRE), 106

RESEARCH: expertise in, influence of, 38–42. *See also* teacher research

RESEARCH COMMUNITY: genesis of, 6–8; members of, 8–13, 11*t*–12*t,* 163; presentations by, 135–137; principles of, 7–8. *See also* large cohort

RESISTANCE: of students, negotiating, 111–112; teacher research and, 144–145

RESPONSE: Bakhtin on, 30

RESPONSIBILITY: concept of, 67–68; definition of, 83; integrating with community and risk, 158–159; K–12 teachers' views of, 135; in large cohort, 133–137; to large cohort, significance of, 139–140; lead investigators' views of, 134; new, taking on, 135–137; rationale for, 89–90; students on, 46–47

RESPONSIBILITY COHORT, 61–90; members of, 11*t,* 163; questions of, 62–64; research topics and data inventory, 165

RICHARDS, I.A., 24

RINGGOLD, F., 81

RISK: integrating with community and responsibility, 158–159; nature of, 119; teacher research community and, 129–131; teachers and, 137–142

RISK COHORT, 91–119; members of, 12*t,* 163; research topics and data inventory, 166

ROGERS, C., 15

ROSENBLATT, L.M., 13, 23–25

RRE. *See* Request-Response-Evaluation

S

SAKAI, R., 21

SALINGER, J.D., 6

SAMUELS, E., 94

SANFORD, B., 15

SARGENT, J., 89

SCHERICK, E.J., 89

SCHRATZ, M., 143

SCHULTZ, K., 65

SCHUMAKER, T., 112

SELF-ASSESSMENT, 107–108; taking responsibility and, 78–82
SELF-INTERROGATION: on social justice, 109–114; space for, 110–111
SELF-QUESTIONING, 4
SELZNICK, D.O., 99
SEXUALITY: classroom treatment and, 94; teacher and, 109–114
SHAKESPEARE, W., 45
SHANNON, P., 66
SHOR, I., 13, 65, 90, 112
SINGER, B.D., 93
SMALL COHORTS, 7; interactions of, 128–129; members of, 9–10, 163; research topics and data inventory, 164–166; tensions in, 38–42
SMITH, R., 100
SOCIAL JUSTICE: self-interrogation on, 109–114
SOCIAL PERSPECTIVES: in classroom, 97–103
SOCKETT, H., 15
SOCRATIC SEMINAR, 45–46; authentic interaction in, 56–57
SOHN, S., 114
SOPHOCLES, 45
SOTO, G., 52
SPEECH AND LANGUAGE DISORDERS: talking detours and, 103–109
SPENCER GROUP, 6–7; members of, 8–13, 11t–12t, 163
SPICER, L., 92
STEWART, J., 15
STONE, P., 89
STRATTON, R., 114
STUDENTS: and classroom agenda, 90; on communication, 104–108; investment in, 14, 159–161; and ownership, 67–68; and taking responsibility, 68–87; and tension, 157–158
SULLIVAN, A.M., 117
SUMNER, G., 55

T

TALKING DETOURS, 103–109; definition of, 105
TAYLOR, M.D., 100
TEACHER(S): and classroom agenda, 90; novice, on teacher research project, 138–139; and ownership, 67–68; and risk, 137–142; and taking responsibility, 68–87; and tension, 157–158; veteran, on teacher research project, 141–142. *See also* K–12 teachers; preservice teachers
TEACHER EDUCATORS: relations with K–12 teachers, 7–8, 17, 126, 132–133, 149–150; roles of, shifting, 156–157; and theory, 21–22
TEACHER RESEARCH: building community for, 128–133; collaborative, framework for, 149–154; novice teachers on, 138–139; publication of, rationale for, 14–15; rationale for, 143–145; topics of, 164–166; veteran teachers on, 141–142; ways of working in, 121–145
TEACHING: from a distance, 65–66; social context of, 44–54
TENSION: and community, 33–59; maintenance of, 157–158; in small cohorts, 38–42
THEORY, 19–31; importance of, 21–23; and research structure, 30–31; unpacking, 23–30
THOMAS, D., 46
THREAT: in critical inquiry classrooms, 110
TIME: for critical inquiry, 148–149; for reflection, 88–89, 140–141

TRANSACTION: and collaboration, 152–153; definition of, 24
TRANSACTIONAL THEORY, 24–26
TRUST: and shared ownership, 75
TYACK, D.B., 96
TYRANNY OF DISTANCE, 131

U

UNDERSTANDING: enduring, 88

V

VETERAN TEACHERS: on teacher research project, 141–142
VYGOTSKY, L.S., 27, 50, 157

W

WALKER, R., 143
WEBSTER'S NINTH NEW COLLEGIATE DICTIONARY, 83
WHITEHEAD, J., 143
WIGGINS, G.P., 88
WILHELM, J.D., 78
WILLIAMS, S., 114
WILLIAMS, T., 20
WONDERING: encouragement of, 52–54

Z

ZEICHNER, K.M., 143
ZONE OF PROXIMAL DEVELOPMENT (ZPD), 55, 157–158